Encouraging Early Spo...

Sandy Green and Jake Green

Contents

Published by Step Forward Limited
St Jude's Church, Dulwich Road, Herne Hill, London, SE24 0PB Tel. 020 7738 5454
© Step Forward Publishing Limited 2008 www.practicalpreschool.com

Encouraging Early Sports Skills ISBN: 9781904575429

Making Plans

Why plan?

The purpose of planning is to make sure that all children enjoy a broad and balanced curriculum All planning should be useful. Plans are working documents that you spend time preparing, which should later repay your efforts. Try to be concise. This will help you in finding information quickly when you need it.

Long-term plans

Preparing a long-term plan, which maps out the curriculum during a year, or even two, will help you to ensure that you are providing a variety of activities and are meeting the statutory requirements of The Early Years Foundation Stage (QCA 2008).

Your long-term plan need not be detailed. Divide the time period over which you are planning into fairly equal sections, such as half-terms. Choose a topic for each section. Young children benefit from making links between the new ideas they encounter so as you select each topic, think about the time of year in which you plan to do it. A topic about minibeasts will not be very successful in November!

Although each topic will address all the learning areas, some could focus on a specific area. For example, a topic on 'Early Sports Skills' would lend itself well to activities relating to Physical Development and Knowledge and Understanding of the World. Another topic might particularly encourage Communication, Language and Literacy. Try to make sure that you provide a variety of topics in your long-term plans. E.g.

Autumn 1	Me and my Family
Autumn 2	Winter
Spring 1	Life cycles
Spring 2	Food and Cooking
Summer 1	Bears
Summer 2	Early Sports Skills

Medium-term plans

Medium-term plans will outline the contents of a topic in a little more detail. One way to start this process is by brainstorming on a large piece of paper. Work with your team writing down all the activities you can think of which are relevant to the topic. As you do this it may become clear that some activities go well together. Think about dividing them into themes. The topic of' Early Sports Skills' for example has themes such as 'Exercise and Health', 'Ball skills', ' Balance and Co-ordination', 'Creative bodies', 'Space and Orientation' and 'Teamwork and co-operation'. At this stage it is helpful to make a chart. Write the theme idea down the side of the chart and put different area of learning at the top of each column. Now you can insert your brainstormed idea enabling you to see where there are gaps. As you complete the chart take account of children's earlier experiences and provide opportunities for them to progress.

Day to day plans

The plans you make for each day will outline aspects such as:
- Resources needed;

The way in which you might introduce activities;
The organisation of adult help;
Size of the group;
Timing;
Key vocabulary.

entify the learning that each activity is intended to promote. Make a note of any assessments
observations that you are likely to carry out. On your plans make notes of activities that were
articularly successful, or any changes you would make another time.

A final note

anning should be seen as flexible. Not all groups meet every day, and not all children attend
very day. Any part of the plan can be used independently, stretched over a longer period or
ondensed to meet the needs of any group. You will almost certainly adapt the activities as
nildren respond to them in different ways and bring their own ideas, interests and enthusiasms.
ne important thing is to ensure that children are provided with a varied and enjoyable
urriculum that meets their individual developing needs.

Using the book

Collect or prepare suggested resources as listed on on pages 58-59.
Read the section which outlines links to the Early Learning Goals (pages 6-9) and explains the
rationale for the topic of 'Early Sports Skills'.
Read through pages 10-29 to refresh your understanding of the requirements of, and
guidelines for, a variety of popular sports. You will find examples of the skills children need to
play these sports included there.
For each weekly theme two activities are described in detail as an example to help you in your
planning and preparation. Key vocabulary, questions and learning opportunities are identified.
The skills chart on page 62 will help you to see at a glance which aspects of children's
development are being addressed as a focus each week.
As children take part in the 'Early Sports Skills' topic activities, their learning will progress.
'Collecting evidence' on on pages 60-61 explains how you might monitor children's achievements.
Find out on page 57 how the topic can be brought together in a grand finale involving
parents, children and friends.
There is additional material to support the working partnership of families and children in the
form of a 'Home links' page, and a photocopiable parents' page at the back of the book.

is important to appreciate that the ideas presented in this book will only be part of your
lanning. Many activities that will be taking place as routine in your group may not be
entioned. For example, it is assumed that sand, dough, water, puzzles, floor toys and large
cale apparatus are part of the on-going preschool experience, as are the opportunities for
nildren to develop ICT skills. Role-play areas, stories, rhymes and singing, and group discussion
mes are similarly assumed to be happening each week, although they may not be a focus for
ne described activities.

When planning the Early Sports Skills topic, remember to take health and safety into account at
ll times. Any new experiences or items of equipment need to be fully risk assessed before use.

Using the Early Learning Goals

Having chosen your topic and made your medium-term plans you can use the Practice Guidance for the Early Years Foundation Stage (QCA 2008) to highlight the key learning opportunities your activities will address. The Early Learning Goals are split into six areas: Personal, Social and Emotional development; Communication, Language and Literacy; Problem Solving, Reasoning and Numeracy; Knowledge and Understanding of the World; Physical Development and Creative Development. Do not expect each of your topics to cover every goal but your long-term plans should allow for all of them to be addressed by the time a child enters Year 1.

The following section highlights parts of the Practice Guidance for the Early Years Foundation Stage in point form to show what children are expected to be able to do in each area of learning by the time they enter Year 1. These points will be used throughout this book to show how activities for a topic on 'Early Sports Skills' link to these expectations. For example, Personal, Social and Emotional development point 3 is 'Maintain attention, concentrate and sit quietly when appropriate'. Activities suggested which provide the opportunity for children to do this will have the reference PS3. This will enable you to see which of the Early Learning Goals are covered in a given week and plan for areas to be revisited and developed.

In addition, you can make sure that activities offer variety in the goals to be encountered. Often a similar activity may be carried out to achieve different learning objectives. For example, during one topic, children may visit a sports field at a local school and look at how different sports activities are played on different surfaces, using different types of 'goal, net, hoop' etc. They will be developing their Knowledge and Understanding of the World. At the same visit they may predict and estimate and take measurements, and feel the weight of 'real' full size sports equipment, therefore building on their problem solving, reasoning and numeracy development.

Personal, Social and Emotional Development

This area of learning covers important aspects of development that affect the way children learn, behave and relate to others.

By the end of the Early Years Foundation Stage, most children will:

PS1   continue to be interested, excited and motivated to learn.
PS2   be confident to try new activities, initiate ideas and speak in a familiar group.
PS3   maintain attention, concentrate, and sit quietly when appropriate.
PS4   respond to significant experiences, showing a range of feelings when appropriate.
PS5   have a developing awareness of their own needs, views and feelings, and be sensitive to the needs, views and feelings of others.
PS6   have a developing respect for their own cultures and beliefs and those of other people.
PS7   form good relationships with adults and peers.
PS8   work as part of a group or class, taking turns and sharing fairly, understanding that there needs to be agreed values and codes of behaviour for groups of people, including adults and children, to work together harmoniously.
PS9   understand what is right, what is wrong, and why.
PS10   consider the consequences of their words and actions for themselves and others.
PS11   dress and undress independently and manage their own personal hygiene.
PS12   select and use activities and resources independently.
PS13   understand that people have different needs, views, cultures and beliefs, that need to be treated with respect.
PS14   understand that they can expect others to treat their needs, views, cultures and beliefs with respect.

'arly Sports Skills' provides an ideal context for children to work towards goals in the Personal, cial and Emotional development area of learning. The team work involved in many sports will :lp children learn to cooperate with others, to listen and respond to the needs of others and consider the outcomes of their own actions and the potential impact on their peers. A sense belonging will develop, helping build confidence and self-esteem. The disciplines involved in ort will help children learn about control, i.e. control of their bodies, control of their behaviour d the need for and benefits of boundaries and rules.

ommunication, Language and Literacy

1e objectives set out in the Primary Framework for Literacy for the Reception year are in line ith these goals. By the end of the Early Years Foundation Stage, most children will be able to:

1   interact with others, negotiating plans and activities and taking turns in conversation.
2   enjoy listening to and using spoken and written language, and readily turn to it in their play and learning.
3   sustain attentive listening, responding to what they have heard with relevant comments, questions or actions.
4   listen with enjoyment, and respond to stories, songs and other music, rhymes and poems and make up their own stories, songs, rhymes and poems.
5   extend their vocabulary, exploring the meanings and sounds of new words.
6   speak clearly and audibly with confidence and control and show awareness of the listener.
7   use language to imagine and recreate roles and experiences.
8   use talk to organise, sequence and clarify thinking, ideas, feelings and events.
9   hear and say sounds in words in the order in which they occur.
10 link sounds to letters, naming and sounding the letters of the alphabet.
11 use their phonic knowledge to write simple regular words and make phonetically plausible attempts at more complex words.
12 explore and experiment with sounds, words and texts.
13 retell narratives in the correct sequence, drawing on language patterns of stories.
14 read a range of familiar and common words and simple sentences independently.
15 know that print carries meaning and, in English, is read from left to right and top to bottom.
16 show an understanding of the elements of stories, such as main character, sequence of events and openings, and how information can be found in non-fiction texts to answer questions about where, who, why and how.
17 attempt writing for different purposes, using features of different forms such as lists, stories and instructions.
18 write their own names and other things such as labels and captions, and begin to form simple sentences, sometimes using punctuation.
19 use a pencil and hold it effectively to form recognisable letters, most of which are correctly formed.

arly Sports Skills' supports children as they move towards attaining the goals in the ommunication, Language and Literacy Development area of learning. They will be interacting ith others as they play sport cooperatively. They will use current and developing vocabulary as 1ey describe and explain positions, intentions and outcomes, and they will share in reflective iscussion of events that have taken place. Children will use mark-making skills to note scores nd list teams and use both spoken and body language to demonstrate, explain and celebrate njoyment and success.

roblem-Solving, Reasoning and Numeracy

he key objectives of Primary Framework for Mathematics are in line with these goals. By the nd of the Early years Foundation Stage, most children should be able to:

N1   say and use number names in order in familiar contexts.
N2   count reliably up to ten everyday objects.
N3   recognise numerals 1 to 9.
N4   use developing mathematical ideas and methods to solve practical problems.
N5   in practical activities and discussion, begin to use the vocabulary involved in adding and subtracting.
N6   use language such as 'more' or 'less' to compare two numbers.
N7   find one more or one less than a number from one to ten.
N8   begin to relate addition to combining two groups of objects and subtraction to 'taking away'.
N9   use language such as 'greater', 'smaller', 'heavier' or 'lighter' to compare quantities.
N10   talk about, recognise and recreate simple patterns.
N11   use language such as 'circle' or 'bigger' to describe the shape and size of solids and flat shapes.
N12   use everyday words to describe position.
N13   use developing mathematical ideas and methods to solve practical problems.

'Early Sports Skills' provides useful opportunities for children to work towards the goals in the Problem Solving, Reasoning and Numeracy Development area of learning. Sport and physical activity involves a great deal of movement, therefore children will be learning to identify and name directions, positions and layouts as they play sport and enjoy physical games. They will be counting numbers of players for small and large teams, calculating how many items of each resource are needed for each particular activity, and solving practical problems such as how to share limited resources and equipment between larger numbers. Pitches and playing courts can be measured and 'marked out', resources can be sorted and classified by features or function, and charts can be produced to record outcomes and numerical data.

Knowledge and Understanding of the World

By the end of the Early Years Foundation Stage, most children will be able to:

K1   investigate objects and materials by using all of their senses as appropriate.
K2   find out about, and identify, some features of living things, objects and events they observe.
K3   look closely at similarities, differences, patterns and change.
K4   ask questions about why things happen and how things work.
K5   build and construct with a wide range of objects, selecting appropriate resources and adapting their work where necessary.
K6   select the tools and techniques they need to shape, assemble and join materials they are using.
K7   find out about and identify the uses of everyday technology and use information and communication technology and programmable toys to support their learning.
K8   find out about past and present events in their own lives, and in those of their families and other people they know.
K9   observe, find out about and identify features in the place they live and the natural world.
K10   find out about their environment, and talk about those features they like and dislike.
K11   begin to know about their own cultures and beliefs and those of other people.

Regarding the goals for the Knowledge and Understanding of the World area of learning, 'Early Sports Skills' provides an ideal context for children to learn more about their world, within both their local and the wider environment. National and international sporting events will provide opportunities to identify where different places are found, either on U.K. and world maps or through the use of a globe. Children can explore and find out about the range of materials that sporting equipment can be made from e.g. leather and synthetic materials for footballs, wood for cricket bats, rubber for balls and hoops, as well as where these materials come from. Technology can be explored through the timing of events, recording of activities and then playing back

ese recordings for reflection and pleasure. Learning about time will be supported through
me-bound games and activities and through exploring sport played by previous generations
g. what might great-granddad have worn when he played football? How different might his
quipment have been? Visits can also be included to local venues e.g. sports arenas, football
adiums, and play areas.

Physical Development (PD)

y the end of the Early Years Foundation Stage, most children will be able to:

D1   move with confidence, imagination and in safety.
D2   move with control and coordination.
D3   travel around, under, over and through balancing and climbing equipment.
D4   show awareness of space, of themselves and of others.
D5   recognise the importance of keeping healthy, and those things which contribute to this.
D6   recognise the changes that happen to their bodies when they are active.
D7   use a range of small and large equipment.
D8   handle tools, objects, construction and malleable materials safely and with increasing
      control.

arly Sports Skills' offers great opportunities for children to work towards goals in the Physical
evelopment area of learning. They will learn to move safely showing understanding of space,
osition and orientation to others, as well as developing control and coordination as they run,
mp, throw, catch and generally enjoy the most obvious physical aspects of learning about
ort. Fine motor-skills will be helped by the use of small equipment such as hoops, bean bags
nd balls, with large motor-skill development being supported through running, jumping,
ipping ropes, use of rackets and bats. Gymnastic and athletic activities will support children
balance and bodily coordination, and good health will be emphasised through discussions of
tness and activity, eating well and looking after their bodies.

Creative Development (C)

y the end of the Early Years Foundation Stage, most children will be able to:

1   respond in a variety of ways to what they see, hear, smell, touch and feel.
2   express and communicate their ideas, thoughts and feelings by using a widening range
     of materials, suitable tools, imaginative and role-play, movement, designing and making,
     and a variety of songs and musical instruments.
3   explore colour, texture, shape, form and space in two or three dimensions.
4   recognise and explore how sounds can be changed, sing simple songs from memory,
     recognise repeated sounds and sound patterns and match movements to music.
5   use their imagination in art and design, music, dance, imaginative and role-play and
     stories.

un activities can be provided during a topic on 'Early Sports Skills', helping children to
ork towards the learning goals in the Creative Development area of learning. There can be
pportunities to record visual images of sport, both the children's own experiences and those
ken from various media. Models of sports venues can be designed and built from 'junk', and
usic can be chosen or composed to accompany 'special' events.

ootball chants can be developed, helping children learn about rhythm, sound patterns and
petition, and children can be creative as they learn 'cheer-leader' routines and support each
thers' 'teams' as they play matches.

Nine Child-Friendly Sports

In this section you will find a brief overview of how to teach children to play each of the following sports:

- Football
- Dodgeball
- Netball and Basketball
- Kwik Cricket
- Rounders
- Short tennis
- Gymnastics
- Athletics

Each sport is accompanid by information on how to set up the game, match, tournament, event or session; the equipment you will need; the basic rules of the sport/event, and the skills needed for, or developed by, each sport. There is also a diagram showing how the players are set out on the pitch, court etc.

Background information on each sport may be beyond the understanding of most children in the Foundation Stage age range, but as adult practitioners it is important to be able to describe what a sport is about, explain relevant rules and be able to use appropriate terminology to name players, positions and equipment. As with all opportunities for learning, as adults we introduce new information and experiences to children in stages, relevant to their age and stage of development. We help them learn new vocabulary and provide activities to help them practice and consolidate skills and actions, which are both directly and indirectly linked to any intended learning outcome.

Football

What is football?

Football is the most popular sport amongst young people in Britain today. It is also the most accessible as there is very little equipment needed for a basic, recreational 'kick about'. All that is essential is the football itself something to depict the goalposts.

In football:

- A professional match lasts for 90 minutes, with a 15 minute half-time break, in which teams change ends for the second half.
- A referee keeps order and makes decisions on foul play.
- The main aim of each team is to score goals, whilst trying not to concede any themselves.
- A team consists of 11 players; 1 goalkeeper and 10 outfield players. However, a match can be played with as few or as many players as space allows, with a minimum of three players on each team.
- Players are sometimes set out in numerical formations e.g. 4-4-2, 4-5-1 etc please see diagram of the football pitch. These are usually chosen according to what skills are needed against particular opposing teams, but in early years settings a numerical formation may be chosen simply to help children understand which combinations of numbers can add up to eleven (or whatever number of players the teams are made up of.)
- Players may use any part of the body other than the arms to strike the ball (Goalkeepers can use their arms as well.)
- Free kicks are given if players are tripped, pushed or pulled back by players from the other team, or if they handle the ball outside of the penalty area. A free kick means that the ball is kicked from where the 'foul' took place.
- A penalty is awarded if a player is tripped, pushed, pulled etc, or handles the ball inside the penalty area. If their handling of the ball has prevented a guaranteed goal, they will also be sent off.
- If the game is stopped for any reason, play is re-started by the referee dropping the ball between two players (one from each team.) The ball must bounce once before players can attempt to take control of it.
- A throw-in is awarded when the ball goes off the pitch (over the side-lines.) It is given to the team that did not put the ball out of play. For a throw-in the ball must be thrown two-handed from behind the throwers head, with both feet touching the floor.
- A goal kick is awarded to the defending team when a player from the attacking team sends the ball over the goal or the 'dead-ball' line. It is usually taken by the goalkeeper, who kicks it as far up the field as they can.
- Players are sent off for any violent conduct e.g. elbowing or kicking at other players instead of the ball.

In setting up a football match with children in the EYFS you will be able to introduce most of the above points in a very simple format. This can be done by playing for shorter periods of time, having as many or as few players on each team as is appropriate, and introducing whichever 'rules' you think the children will be able to understand and respond to, taking into account their ages and stages of development. If football is played regularly, you will be able to introduce additional rules from time to time, building on both the sports knowledge and the physical skills of the children.

Skills and attributes needed

Goalkeepers need:

- Strength.
- The ability to jump.
- Good hand-eye coordination to help them prevent goals being scored.
- Good foot-eye coordination to enable them to kick the ball in the direction they intend.
- To be unafraid of the ball or of physical contact.

All other (outfield) players need:

- Good spatial awareness, e.g. being aware of where other players in their team are, being ready to pass or accept the ball from them.
- Good ball control e.g. having the ability to keep and manoeuvre the ball when it is in their possession.
- Good foot-eye control for judging direction, distance and the amount of power required.
- Good overall fitness levels as football involves a great deal of running.
- The ability to pass the ball accurately i.e. judging both direction and distance.
- Good orientation skills e.g. an awareness of what is going on around them.
- The ability to concentrate and follow instructions.
- The ability to tackle other players to regain the ball.

Equipment

- A football.
- Four cones to use as goalposts.
- Different coloured bibs or sashes can also be useful to distinguish between the teams.

How to set up a football pitch

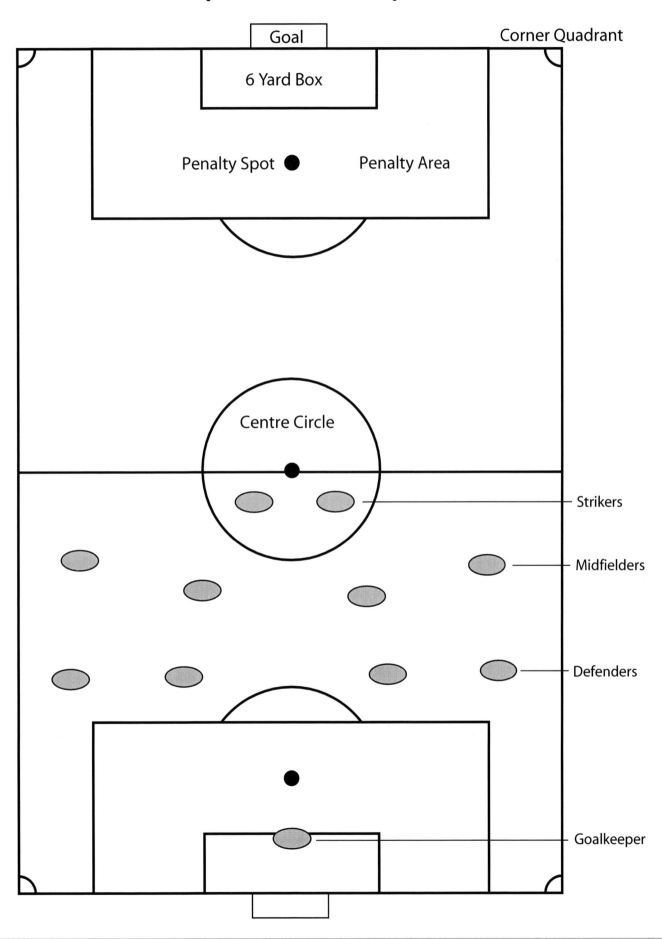

Goal

Corner Quadrant

6 Yard Box

Penalty Spot ● Penalty Area

Centre Circle

Strikers

Midfielders

Defenders

Goalkeeper

Dodgeball

What is dodgeball?

The sport of dodgeball consists of players moving around the playing court trying to avoid being hit by balls that are being aimed at them by the opposing team. In dodgeball:

- There are two teams of six players (although anywhere between 4 and 8 players on each team would also work well.)
- Players must remain in their own half of the court throughout the game.
- There is a marked out playing area (the court.) In professional games this measures 30m x 12-15m, but in early years settings adults need to simply ensure that children have sufficient room to move around safely. There needs to be a dividing line across the centre of the court.
- There are six balls in use throughout the game, which are initially set along the centre-line of the court. Only soft sponge balls that will not hurt on contact should be used in early years settings.
- Players run to the centre-line to get a ball when the match begins.
- Each team throws balls at the opposing team members. No kicking of the balls, or use of any body part except the hands is permitted. Balls must only be directed at the chest or lower body, never at the face or head.
- Players who are hit by a ball are considered to be out of the game.
- Players who catch a ball cause the opposing team player who threw the ball to be out of the game, and one of their own team members can return to the game in their place. This would usually be the player who has been out on the sidelines the longest, ensuring a fair rotation of players.
- Any player holding a ball can block any other ball thrown at them (although this strategy will be too advanced for most children in the EYFS.)

Skills needed

- The ability to catch a ball.
- The ability to aim and throw a ball, judging both distance and direction.
- Agility to enable players to 'dodge' out of the way of balls aimed at them.
- With older children, strategies of playing as a pair or as a whole team can be used to tactically isolate and eliminate opposing players, but this strategy will be too advanced for most children in the EYFS.

Equipment

- Six soft sponge balls
- A clearly divided court
- The wearing of coloured bibs may help the youngest children avoid confusing their own players with the opposing team as the players gradually get closer to the dividing line in the centre.

How to set up a dodgeball court

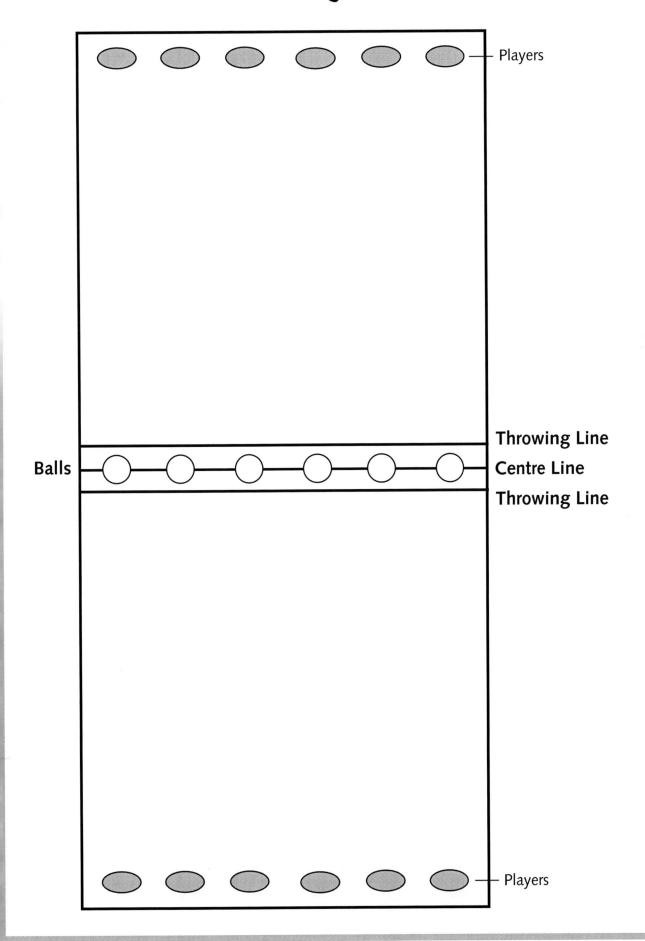

Players

Throwing Line

Balls   Centre Line

Throwing Line

Players

Netball and Basketball

Netball and basketball have many similarities in the sense that they are both non-contact sports and both involve passing a ball by hand with the ultimate goal of shooting the ball through a hoop at the end of the court.

What is netball?

In netball :

- There are two teams of seven players who each have their own playing position. These positions are Goal Keeper (GK), Goal Defence (GD), Wing Defence (WD), Centre (C), Wing Attack (WA), Goal Attack (GA) and Goal Shooter (GS).
- The playing court is divided into thirds, a 'centre third' sandwiched between two 'goal thirds', with a D shaped area in both of the goal thirds and restrictions on which players are allowed in each section.
- A match is divided into four quarters, each lasting fifteen minutes.
- Each team tries to put as many balls through the hoop (goals) at the opposite end of the court as they can.
- The ball must always pass through each third of the court. It must never pass directly from goal third to goal third.
- Players pass the ball on to another player without taking more than one step.

What is basketball?

In basketball :

- There is a much faster playing pace than in netball.
- There are two teams of twelve players, of which only five players are on the court at any one time. This is because of the fast pace of the game.
- All players are allowed to travel anywhere on the court.
- The ball must stay within the boundaries of the court at all times.
- No player is allowed to be in contact with the ball and the outside of the court at the same time.
- Once caught the ball must either be passed, or continually bounced with one hand in order to 'dribble' it along the court.
- The aim is to try and score as many 'baskets' (goals) as each player can.
- Players must pass the ball on, or start 'dribbling', within 5 seconds of receiving the ball.

Skills needed for both sports

- The ability to catch a ball.
- The ability to aim and throw a ball, judging both distance and direction.
- The ability to pass a ball from one player to the other.
- The ability to bounce a ball with a degree of control.
- An awareness of space is particularly needed in basketball.
- The ability to move safely at speed.
- Hand-eye coordination to enable them to score a goal or basket.

- Cooperation with other players.
- A good level of general fitness.

Equipment

- For netball, ideally there will be small hoop at each end of the court, together with a netball (a large sponge ball will be ideal), plus coloured bibs for each team (bibs with playing positions are useful for older children, but not needed when playing with children in the EYFS).
- For basketball, there needs to be a suitably marked out basketball court. Plus a basket ball (a ball that bounces well is needed), and coloured bibs for younger children to help them easily identify their own team mates.

How to set up a netball court

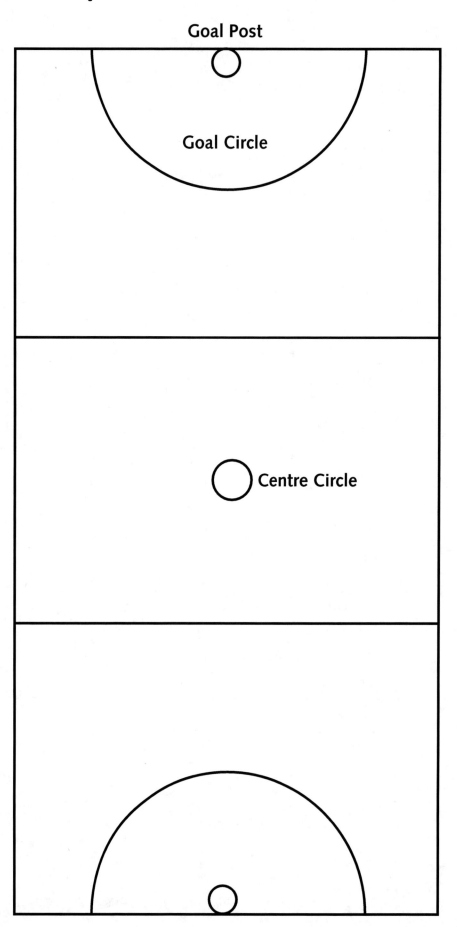

Goal Post

Goal Circle

Centre Circle

Encouraging Early Sports Skills

How to set up a basketball court

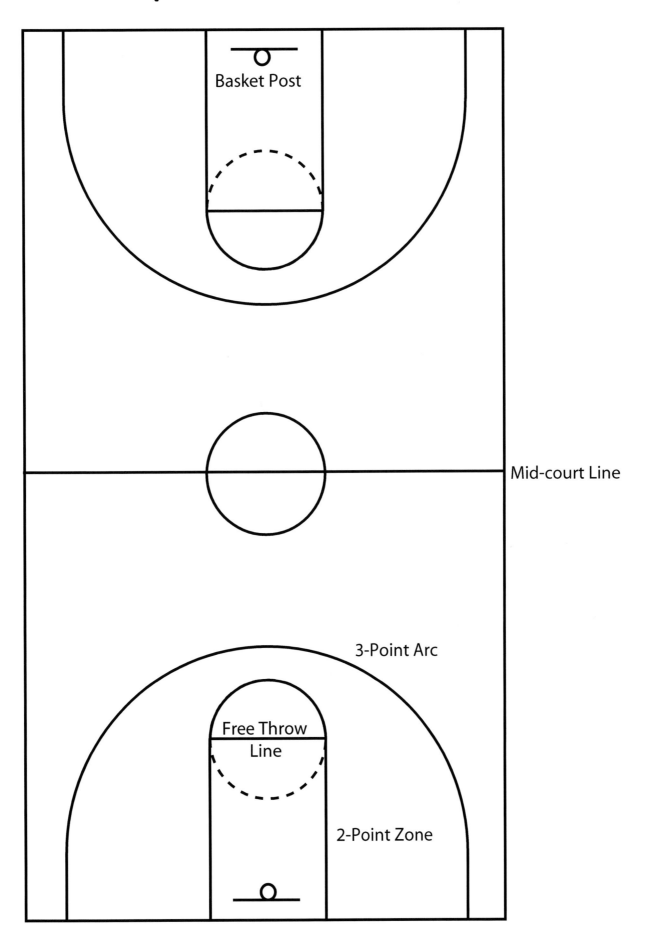

Basket Post

Mid-court Line

3-Point Arc

Free Throw Line

2-Point Zone

Kwik Cricket

What is kwik cricket?

In primary schools a simple form of the main 'professional rules' game is usually played. In Kwik Cricket:

- There is only one batsman playing at a time who stands in front of his/her wicket.
- Also, there is one bowler who stands approximately twelve metres away (a much shorter distance will be needed when playing with children in the EYFS), and who bowls underarm at the stumps (also called the wicket).
- All the other players are fielders who try to 'catch out' the batsman or get the ball back to the bowler as quickly as possible.
- There can be as few as five players, or as many as fifteen, depending on the size of the playing area.
- The batsman runs to a second wicket (positioned to the left of his/her wicket) and back again each time the ball is bowled to them, whether s/he has hit the ball or not.
- The bowler tries to 'bowl' or 'catch' out the batsman.
- The batsman tries to score as many 'runs' as possible.

Skills and attitudes needed

- Good hand-eye coordination to enable the bowler and fielders to catch the ball and the batsman to hit balls bowled to them.
- The ability to throw and catch a ball, judging speed, distance and direction.
- Good levels of fitness as there is plenty of running involved.

Equipment

- A set of wickets
- A cricket bat
- A soft ball

How to set up a kwik cricket pitch

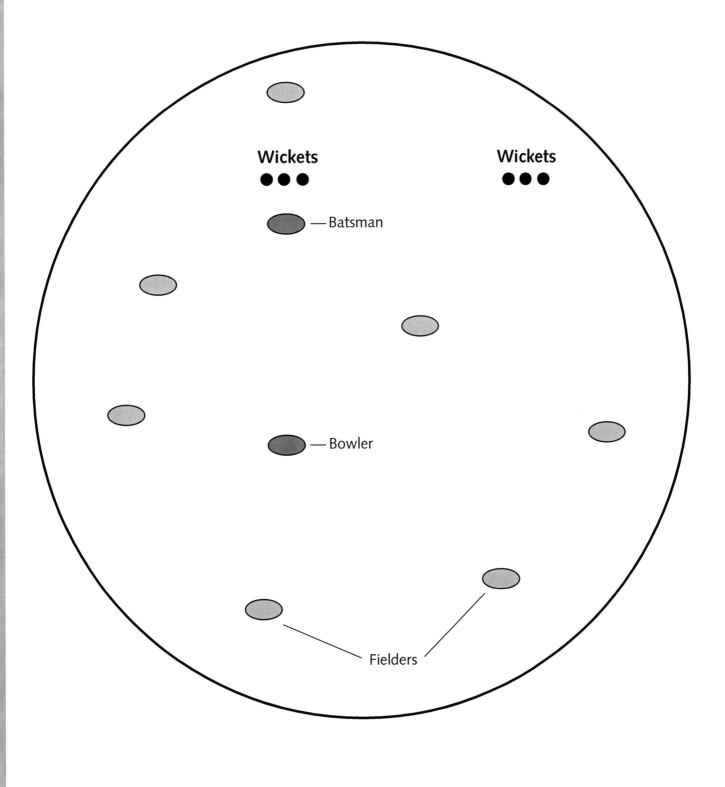

Wickets
Wickets
— Batsman
— Bowler
Fielders

Rounders

A rounders game

Rounders is a game loosely based on the American game of baseball. It can easily be played by adults and children of all ages. In rounders:

- There are two teams of six to fifteen players.
- Teams take turns to bat and to field.
- The playing area is set out roughly as a square.
- The playing time is called an 'innings'.
- The aim is for each team to score as many rounders as they can i.e. hit the ball as far as they can and then run without stopping round all four posts back to the hitting area.
- Batters can stop at the 'posts' if they do not have time to get all the way round, but only one batter can be at a post at any one time.
- The batter must drop the bat before they run.
- Batters are caught out if they do not reach the next post before the ball hits it.
- The batter stands in the hitting area whilst players waiting their turn to bat wait in the 'waiting' area.
- The bowler bowls the ball underarm with both feet inside the 'pitching' area.
- The ball must not bounce before it reaches the batter and should arrive within the batter's reach i.e. above knee and below head height.
- Once the batter has hit the ball they run to the first 'post'. They run round as many 'posts' as possible before the ball is hit against a post by a fielder, or is returned to the bowler.
- The fielding players try to catch the batters out whenever they can.
- The winning team is the team with the most rounders.
- The game is usually played until all players are 'out', but a time limit can easily be set for each team to be either batters or fielders.

Skills needed

- Good hand-eye coordination to enable successful hitting of the ball, catching of the ball and the ability to hit the four posts.
- The ability to hit a ball, judging both distance and direction.
- A good level of general fitness, as playing rounders involves a great deal of running.
- An understanding of the need to run as soon as the ball is hit if stopped at one of the posts.

Equipment

- When playing rounders with children in the EYFS, it should ideally be played on grass or an impact absorbent surface. The pitch needs to be clearly marked out.
- A rounders bat, which is long and straight.
- A ball. Traditional rounders' balls are made of stitched leather, but a medium sized, soft rubber ball is much more suitable for young children.
- Items to denote the four 'posts' on the playing field. Tall, solid cones would be ideal, or alternatively, large milk containers, cleaned and filled with sand or water.

How to set up a rounders pitch

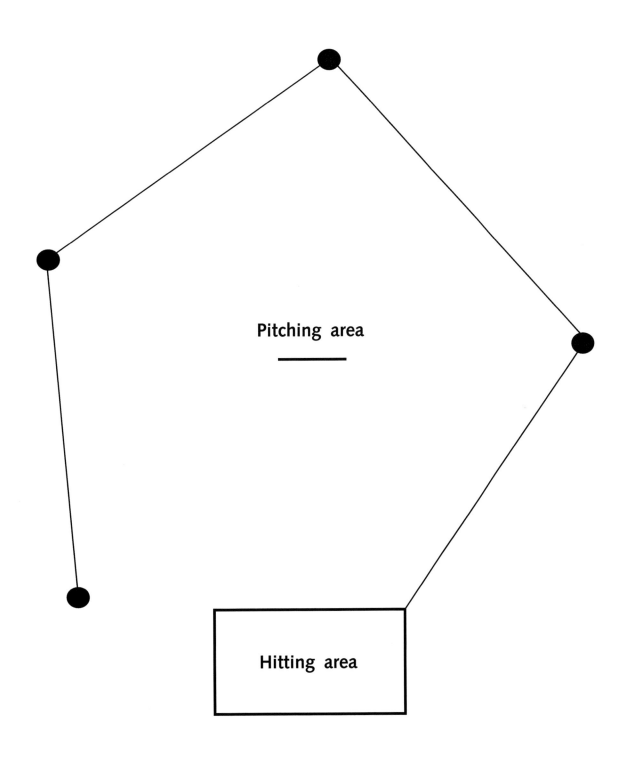

Pitching area
———

Hitting area

Short tennis

What is short tennis?

Short tennis is mostly played indoors. It is a simplified version of the conventional game. In short tennis:

- There can be either two players (singles) or four players (doubles).
- They use a squishy rubber ball, much softer than a traditional lawn tennis ball, enabling a game based around longer passages of play (rallies), rather than the more powerful shots seen in professional lawn tennis matches where it is more difficult to return the ball.
- The ball is 'served' into the area of the court which is diagonally opposite.
- Players lose a point to their opponent if they hit the net, or if they hit the ball out of court.
- The first player to reach 4 points wins the game, and the first player to win 4 games wins the match (with a margin of at least 2 games e.g. 4-2 or 5-3).

Skills needed

- Good hand-eye coordination to enable players to visually track and then hit the ball.
- Good general physical coordination to enable players to plan for, and respond to, the direction, pace and power of the ball.
- Agility to enable players to move easily around the court.
- A good level of general fitness.

Equipment

- A marked out playing court with a net.
- A racket of a size suitable for the individual size of the player.
- A squishy rubber ball (not a tennis ball).

How to set up a tennis court

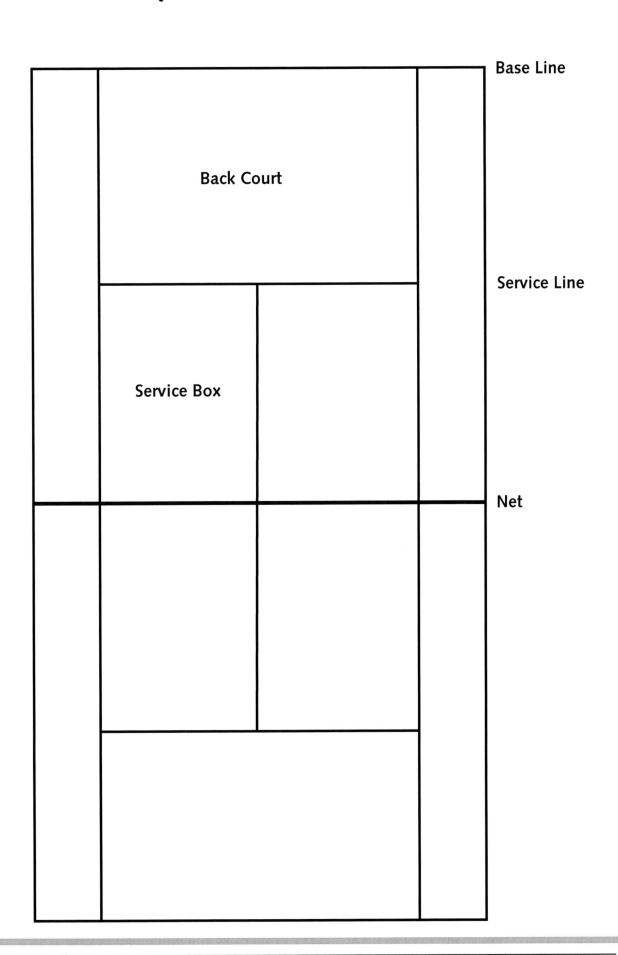

Base Line

Service Line

Net

Back Court

Service Box

Gymnastics

What does gymnastics involve?

Males and females compete separately in gymnastics events although some disciplines are alike, and demonstrate a similar range of skills. The following disciplines are the ones mostly seen televised during national, international and world events. Gymnastics takes place on a range of equipment for example:

- A sprung-floor
- A vaulting horse
- Balance beams
- Asymmetric bars
- The pommel horse
- The high bar
- The still rings

As with all aspects of learning it is important to show children within the EYFS examples of a range of gymnastics equipment being used, to help put into context some of the skills they are learning. Of course, in early years settings any 'gymnastics' activities are likely to be limited to the use of items such as impact absorbent mats for jumps, rolls and rhythmic dance routines, and a low bench to support the development of balance.

Gymnastics can also involve:
- Aerobic gymnastics which focuses on strength, flexibility and aerobic fitness. Short routines are performed on a small floor area.
- Rhythmic gymnastics which involves the use of creative resources; ribbons, hoops, balls, clubs or rope. Routines are performed to music on a floor area. The main focus of this is aesthetic rather than acrobatic.
- Tumbling and trampolining, either as individuals or as synchronised pairs. These disciplines involve achieving height, together with a range of twists and tumbles.
- Acrobatic gymnastics in which groups of up to four gymnasts perform routines to music, involving the hands, feet and heads of their partners.
- Team gymnastics in which a series of tumbles and vaults are carried out over three disciplines: tumbling, floor and trampette. Team members demonstrate flexibility, acrobatic skills and skilful choreography, all carried out to music.

Skills needed

- Hand-eye coordination
- Foot-eye coordination
- Spatial awareness
- Strength
- Coordination
- Flexibility
- Ability to jump and land safely.
- Ability to balance on different body parts.
- Ability to move from one position to another in safety and with control.
- Ability to synchronise actions with another person.
- Ability to remain still, and to stop and move as directed.

Equipment

In early years settings suitable equipment to support early gymnastics activities will include:

- Impact-absorbent mats for jumps, rolls and to support general safety.
- Planks and low benches for balancing activities and routines involving controlled transference of weight, or travelling in a coordinated manner.
- Ribbons, balls, hoops etc. for rhythmic routines.
- Other small apparatus for marking out boundaries may also be used e.g. cones or carpet squares.

Athletics

What is included in athletics?

Athletics includes both track events such as sprint racing, long-distance racing, hurdling and relay racing, and field events such as long jump, high jump, triple jump, pole vault, javelin, shot-put and hammer. In competitions females sometimes complete a series of seven events known as the heptathlon and males complete a series of ten events known as the decathlon. In introducing athletics to young children:

- Ensure that the chosen events will be safe, easily controlled by the supervising adults, and fun.
- Ensure that the events selected are manageable for the space available and the numbers of children.
- Ensure that the skills and interests of all children are provided for.
- Use prior observations of children's physical skills to identify where additional support is likely to be needed for certain children.
- Plan to offer extension opportunities for the more physically able children.
- Ensure that you have appropriate adult supervision at all times.
- Ensure that risk assessments have been carried out for all activities.

Skills needed

- An awareness of space, direction and orientation to ensure safe running.
- Good foot-eye coordination to help avoid tripping accidents when taking part in hurdling events.
- Good hand-eye coordination and the ability to throw, judging distance and direction.
- The ability to keep a steady pace and rhythm to enable successful hurdling and relay racing.
- The ability to jump both forwards (long jump) and upwards (high jump).
- An awareness of how to position the body for certain actions e.g. for the push style throw used in shot-put with beanbags, and for the handover of a 'baton' in relay racing.

Equipment

When setting up athletic events with children in the EYFS you are likely to need:

- A clear safe area for running, if possible marked into 'lanes'. This can be used for sprint racing, hurdling and relay racing.
- Resources to be used as hurdles e.g. lines of small cones positioned along the 'running track' at regular intervals.
- A wall that children can be measured against with their arms stretched fully upwards. A length of paper is then secured to the wall starting at the tips of their fingers. The child then jumps upwards against the wall and positions a piece of Blu Tack to the paper. It can then be easily seen how high each child has jumped. Although very different from the traditional high jump event this method is far safer for young children than jumping over a bar and also has the benefit of offering no advantage or disadvantage to taller or shorter children.

- Beanbags and medium-sized sponge balls to use in place of javelins, shot-puts and hammers which are clearly not suitable for children to use.
- Batons (slim plastic skittles or empty water bottles could be an alternative) for use during relay events.
- A sandpit clear of toys and equipment, which has been raked smooth to use as a long jump or triple jump pit. Alternatively, impact absorbent mats can be used, or soft grassy areas. Be aware of how hard grass can become in dry weather.
- See following illustration for how to set up this high jump for the early years.

How to set up a high jump

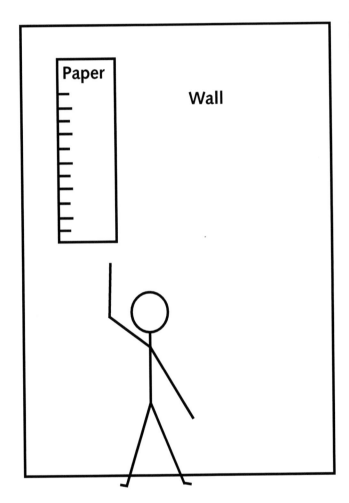

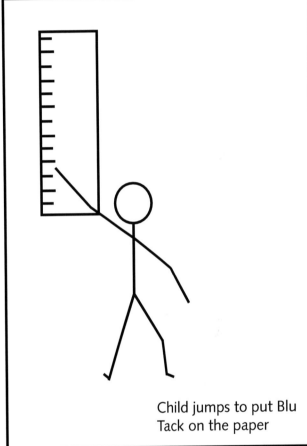

Child jumps to put Blu Tack on the paper

Developing Physical Skills for Sport

As children build on both their gross and fine physical skills through the sporting and sport-linked activities set out in this book they will also be learning the disciplines of co-operation, negotiation, self-control and teamwork. They will be using listening skills and concentration, and will have opportunities to initiate, replicate, lead and follow. They will put sport into various relevant contexts and explore sport in the wider environment. This shows how sport and physical activity can play an important part in a child's all-round development.

Young children need opportunities to develop both their gross motor-skills and their fine motor-skills (manipulation). Development starts as soon as an infant begins to touch and explore their environment e.g. the surface of a brick, a teddy or shaker, the movement of a mobile, balloon or wind chime. They learn about space and orientation as they observe others within their environment, experience what is within and out of their reach, and locate familiar people by sound

Children need a range of different resources that provide a variety of challenges and experiences and which interest them and motivate them to explore further. Activities which support the development of fine motor skills include:

- Drawing, writing and general mark-making resources.
- Using computers and keyboards.
- Puzzles, posting and stacking toys and any type of construction material.
- Sewing, threading, weaving.
- Use of malleable materials such as clay, dough, sand and water.
- Handling of balls, beanbags, hoops, quoits, skipping ropes etc.

Large motor development includes both locomotor skills i.e. actions involving moving forward in some way such as hopping, jumping, running, and non-locomotor skills where the action does not involve moving forwards e.g. bending, pushing, pulling. Large motor development is supported through the following opportunities:

- Climbing and balancing, movement sessions, (with or without music.)
- Crawling through tunnels, bouncing on trampettes.
- Cycling and using scooters.
- Learning to walk along a chalk line or narrow beam.
- Stepping from carpet square to carpet square, playing ring games, enjoying action rhymes and active games such as hopscotch.

Movement, dance and gym sessions encourage children to develop the skills they need in order to jump, skip, glide, bounce, leap, roll, spin and run safely within a controlled environment. They also provide opportunities to practice balance skills, sequencing, creative expression and general body control.

Stages of Physical Development

Development takes place in stages, moving from the simple to the more complex. For example, an infant needs to be able to hold up their head with a degree of control before they are able to sit unsupported. They need to be able to sit before they can stand, and to stand before they can walk

Many of the core skills needed for sport and gymnastic activities develop through three main stages, often referred to as the immature, intermediate and mature stages. For example:

- Toddlers tend to fall into a football when they try to kick it (immature stage), when a little older they kick a ball from a set position (intermediate stage), and eventually they will be able to kick the ball with power, using the natural arm and body swings that provide the momentum needed (mature stage.)
- When trying to catch a ball, a toddler initially averts their face whilst holding their arms out straight and will simply pull the ball to their chest (immature stage), often with little success. When a little older they hold their arms less rigidly and avert their face less, but still have limited success (intermediate stage). Finally they use hand-eye coordination to track the ball as it comes towards them, grasping it with greater levels of success (mature stage).

Crossing the midline

Another significant physical stage children need to reach in order for many sporting and gymnastic skills to be fully developed is that of 'crossing the midline'. This is where a child can reach across their body (in which arms and legs cross from one side of the body to the other) as part of their natural movement and actions. Some children do however continue to find this difficult. Activities to help them develop this important 'skill' include:

- Drawing a large figure of eight on the ground and asking the children to walk continuously around it.
- As a group drawing imaginary (sideways) figure of eights in the air with your finger or arm.
- Asking children to pick up small items positioned to one side of them, using the opposite hand.
- Providing plenty of fine motor skills activities as mentioned before.

Preparation for physical activity

As you plan physical activities it is important to:

- Ensure the personal safety of both children and adults e.g. long hair tied back, jewellery removed, all participants wearing suitable clothing and footwear, with bare feet whenever practical for indoor movement, dance and gymnastic activities.
- Check that all equipment to be used is safely positioned, well maintained, clean, and has been risk assessed.
- Ensure that there is sufficient space for the numbers of participating children to work safely.
- Incorporate time for children to 'warm up' their bodies before the main activity commences and to cool their bodies down again afterwards. This is sometimes referred to as 'warming down'.

Warm-up exercises

Encouraging children to warm up and cool down helps to loosen up children's bodies, enabling them to progress further with physical activities, and can also help prevent the overstretching of muscles and ligaments. Warm up exercises could include:

- Gentle stretching of arms and legs followed by stretching of the whole body.
- Gentle running on the spot, on their toes, on the balls of the feet etc.
- Throwing and catching a ball 'on the spot'.
- Moving slowly around the room in different ways without touching anyone else.
- Balancing briefly on different parts of the body e.g. on one leg, on their back with their legs in the air, on their bottom with legs tucked into their body etc.

Part of a warm-up can also include getting children to reflect on past activities and recalling the skills and disciplines that were needed.

Warm down / Cooling down exercises

Depending on what activity has taken place many of the above suggestions can also help cool the body down again. It can also be good to encourage children to demonstrate a skill, activity or achievement to the rest of the group. This places value on what they have done, helps build self-esteem and, if the physical session has been fast, loud and/or excitable can be particularly useful in preparing children for the next part of the day.

Developing relevant skills

The sports in the previous section include the need for children to develop the following skills and attitudes. Some will apply only to specific sports, but many apply to all sports. They include having:

- The ability to jump
- Good hand-eye coordination
- Good foot-eye coordination
- Good general body coordination
- A lack of fear of being hit by a ball
- Spatial awareness
- Good ball control
- The ability to pass a ball accurately, judging direction and distance
- The ability to catch a ball
- The ability to aim and throw a ball
- The ability to bounce a ball
- Awareness of space, direction and orientation
- The ability to concentrate and follow instructions
- The ability to tackle other players to gain the ball
- Understanding of how to co-operate with other team members
- The ability to balance on different parts of the body
- The ability to move safely at speed
- The ability to jump and land safely
- The ability to move from one position to another safely and with control
- The ability to synchronise actions with another person
- The ability to remain still, and to stop and move as directed
- The ability to keep and respond to a steady pace and rhythm
- The ability to jump both forwards and upwards
- An awareness of how to position the body for certain actions
- Agility
- Strength
- Good general fitness
- Flexibility

Many of these skills can be practiced through the following activities:

Activity 1
Provide beanbags for each child and encourage them to throw them up and catch them again whilst standing still.

Activity 2
Provide one beanbag for every two children and encourage them to work in pairs throwing and catching.

Activity 3
Set hoops out along the floor and provide a large quantity of beanbags. Encourage children to throw the beanbags into a hoop from behind a chalked line. Gradually increase the distance they are needing to throw, or mark out three chalk lines initially and ask the children to decide which line they start from, helping them reflect on whether they need to move closer or try to throw from further away.

Activity 4

Set up a 'netball' type hoop and provide each child with a beanbag. Encourage the children to throw their beanbags up and through the hoops. Try this also with balls of different sizes.

Activity 5

Set up a simple obstacle course using cones. Position a box at the far end and give each child a pile of beanbags. Let them practice running in and out of the cones to drop the beanbags in the box. This can also be set up as a simple relay-style race.

Activity 6

Give each child a large ball and show them how to pat it to make it bounce on the ground in front of them and then catch it again. Who can bounce it more than once before catching it?

Activity 7

Position the children in a large circle, one behind the other. Allow for plenty of space between each child. Give each child a large ball and encourage them to bounce and catch as they walk slowly clockwise round the circle. As their skills develop either a) encourage them to move more quickly. Who can still keep control of their bouncing ball? Or b) divide the children into smaller groups according to how their bouncing skill is developing. Set the more able children to move at a faster pace than those still developing their skill.

Activity 8

In pairs or small groups encourage the children to bounce a large ball to each other. How many times can the ball bounce before they are unable to catch it any more?

Activity 9

In pairs or small groups, sit on the floor with feet apart and roll a ball to each other. Provide balls of different sizes. Which do they find easiest to control and why?

Activity 10

In pairs ask the children to kick a large ball to each other, always aiming to stop and return the ball with their feet. The aim is for them not to use their hands at all.

Activity 11

Using cones or something similar, set out a zigzag style obstacle course and encourage the children to 'dribble' a large ball in and out of the zigzags with their feet, keeping control of the ball all the time.

Activity 12

Using the zigzagged cones as in activity 11, encourage the children to bounce a large ball as they weave in and out of the cones. At the far end set up a 'basket' or hoop. Who can 'dribble' the ball all the way, and score a 'basket'?

Activity 13

Place a set of skittles in the traditional 4-3-2-1 formation. Using a chalk line as their starting point, encourage the children to 'bowl' a medium-sized ball along the ground to knock over as many skittles as they can. As with activity 3, gradually increase the distance the ball needs to travel.

Activity 14

In pairs initially, and then in small groups, encourage children to throw and catch balls of different sizes. As their skills develop encourage them to try this one-handed, using both left and right hand.

Activity 15

If you have a small goal net, set it up. Alternatively, mark out a goal with cones or something similar. Again, draw a chalk-line which the children must not cross. The aim is to kick a large ball from behind the line to score a goal. Encourage children to try this from different angles and also encourage them to take a 'running kick'. Most children will use the same foot each time, so as their skill develops encourage them to try using their other foot too.

Activity 16

In chalk, mark out a 'target' on a flat wall. Again, from behind a chalk line, see who can throw a ball and hit the target. The target could have more than one circle, with higher 'scores' gained for hitting the smaller (inner) circles.

Activity 17

Provide each child with a racket or bat, together with a ball. Who can toss the ball gently up in the air with their racket, 'catching' it again on their racket? How many times can they do this without losing control of the ball?

Activity 18

Provide each child with a racket or bat, and a ball. Who can bounce their ball up and down on the floor with their racket? How many times can they do this before losing control?

Activity 19

Set up a net or tie a rope firmly between two posts. Using rackets and balls, encourage the children to practice hitting the balls over the net. As their skill develops, set them up in pairs to hit the ball to each other.

Activity 20

Set out large hoops on the ground, initially one for each child. The aim is for the children to jump in and out of their hoop keeping both feet together, without moving the hoop. As their skill develops, set the hoops out in rows of five, with space to jump in between each hoop too. Play 'follow the leader' jumping in and out of the hoops as a team.

Activity 21

Provide each child with a skipping rope and let them practice the skills needed to 'turn rope'. Ensure that ropes are of suitable lengths for the height of the children.

Activity 22

Set out a range of carpet squares for the children to move across. Encourage them to explore different ways of moving from square to square. Suggestions could include: jumping, hopping, leaping with knees in the air, using alternate feet, springing 'bunny hop' style.

Activity 23

Set up a simple obstacle course that will encourage children to practice a sequence of different body movements using, for example :

- A low bench for children to step onto, run along and jump off
- A tunnel to travel through
- A mat to perform three star-jumps on
- A hoop to get their whole body through
- A narrow beam (or line of wide tape) to balance along.

Activity 24

Provide coloured 'tags' for each child to tuck into the top of their shorts. The aim of the activity is for the children to move around the room without bumping in to anyone else, but to get close enough to 'catch' tags from other children. How many tags can they each collect?

Activity 25

Provide ribbons, streamers, scarves and pom-poms and encourage children to move and dance, using the resources to inspire them. Once they have explored how their chosen resource responds to various actions, help them to devise their own dance or sequence of movements to music.

Activity 26

Using a parachute, or large piece of lightweight material, encourage the children to move the parachute in time with each other, up and down, up and down. Take it in turns for the children to run underneath and then out the other side, rejoining those holding the edges of the parachute, e.g. first the boys, then all the girls.

Encouraging Early Sports Skills

Week 1 Exercise and Health

Personal, Social and Emotional development

■ During circle time talk about fitness and exercise. Who can explain what these terms mean? Discuss how exercise is important for healthy development and how it is part of their bodies' needs. What exercises can they describe? When have they seen people exercising? How much exercise do they get? Do they play outside? Do they ride bikes? Do they go to the park, to dancing classes, gymnastics etc? (PS5)

■ Take opportunities whenever you can to discuss healthy and not-so-healthy foods. Introduce new foods at snack times and encourage each child to try something they haven't tried before. Share ideas about why they are considered good foods for us all to eat and encourage the children to think of other aspects of their lives that can have an impact on their health and well-being. (PS1)

■ Talk to the children about different ways of keeping clean and the importance of careful hand washing. Help them to understand how cross-infection can occur if germs are not washed from their hands after using the toilet, blowing their noses etc. (PS11)

Communication, Language and Literacy

■ Introduce children to the internal organs of the body. Help them to learn their proper names e.g. heart, muscles, kidneys. Explain simply what each organ does to keep the body working properly and how the children can help it function. Make links to food, cleanliness and keeping fit, encouraging and answering questions and acknowledging the suggestions and observations they make. (L3)

■ Sing action songs such as "The head bone's connected to the neck bone ..." etc. Use a visual image of a skeleton to help the children see how the body is built up and use gesture and body actions to demonstrate understanding. Read books such as *Funnybones* by Janet and Allan Ahlberg. (L4)

■ Introduce vocabulary associated with exercising. Include terms such as hot, puffed, breathless, gasp, sweaty etc. (L5)

■ Set up a game of basketball and rotate the children who are playing at any one time. The children will need to listen carefully for their names to be called, and respond quickly. (L3)

Problem Solving, Reasoning and Numeracy

■ Encourage the children to count each others body parts – arms, legs, fingers, toes, eyes, ears etc. Help them to discover symmetry by looking at how they are all even numbers and are found in matching pairs/sets on each side of the body. Use a full-length mirror to help children observe symmetry in themselves. (N2)

■ Take turns in balancing on first one leg and then the other. Count how long each person can hold their balance, or use a timer. Help the children to make a line graph to show their best times. (N10)

■ Enjoy a jumping and hopping session together. Provide a bar chart on which each child can plot its highest number of jumps or hops without stopping. Encourage the children to identify who else hopped or jumped the same number of times as themselves, and who achieved more or less than themselves. How can they show that information on the bar chart? To help the children see how they are developing the 'spring' needed to jump up high, set up a high-jump activity against a wall. (N6)

Knowledge and Understanding of the World

■ Show children where to find their pulse. This is not always easy to do, so plenty of time and patience will be needed. Explain that their pulse indicates how fast their heart is beating. An illustration will be helpful in ensuring they see the connection. Provide equipment such as a stethoscope for them to listen to each other's heartbeats. Measure your own pulse before carrying out some form of exercise, e.g. jumping, hopping, skipping, running on the spot, and then measure it again afterwards. Talk to the children about how it differs and how you are feeling. Ask them how different they feel when they have been running fast. Take them to a suitable area for them to try this out. Explain the connection between being out of breath and the change in their pulse rate. (K1)

■ Use media articles and, if possible, food advertisements, to produce an information booklet or display on well-known sportsmen and women the children are familiar with. Include how each sportstar might keep themselves fit and healthy: what foods they would mostly eat, and what sorts of exercise they would do. (K8)

Physical Development

■ Use beanbags or small tins of food as weights and do some simple exercises. Ask the children to describe what they feel and where they are experiencing any new feelings. Always encourage children to stretch and bend their bodies gently before and after exercise. This will teach them the relevance of 'warming up' and 'cooling down' the body. Ensure that you do not let children over-exert themselves. (PD6)

■ Set up a low bench or find a place of a similarly low height, such as a long step, and take turns to practice 'step ups'. As with the above suggestion, ask the children to explain where they can feel the effects of the exercise. Again, always include some simple stretches and bends to warm the body up and cool it down again. (PD5)

■ Plan a simple routine of three exercises and make a short exercise video together. Start the video with a warm up exercise and end it with a cooling down exercise. (PD2)

Creative Development

■ Make a skeleton together using stiff card and enable the joints to 'move' by using crocodile clips or straws (see activity opposite). (C2)

■ Provide materials for each child to draw a large picture of themselves and help them to add picture or word labels to show their understanding of where each of their main body parts can be found. (C5)

■ Set up a wall display on healthy and not-so-healthy foods. Use food packaging and pictures from magazines, supermarket pamphlets etc. to illustrate. Let the children paint pictures or create images of their favourite foods and help them identify whether they should be added to the healthy foods display or the not-so-healthy foods. Avoid using the term 'unhealthy' as many children will have a less than ideal diet at home and it is important not to seem to make direct value judgements on their families' choices. (C3)

Making skeletons activity

Learning opportunity: Finding out about our bodies.

Early Learning Goal: Knowledge and Understanding of the World. The children will be finding out and identifying some features of living things, and selecting tools and techniques to shape, assemble, and join materials they are using.

Resources: Books such as *Funnybones* by Janet and Allen Ahlberg, a large visual image (e.g. a poster) showing the bones of a skeleton, card, scissors, crocodile clips, stapler and staples, string, sticky tape, craft straws, pens and pencils.

Key vocabulary: Names of the bones e.g. thigh, pelvis, ribs, skull etc.

Organisation: In small groups of three or four children.

What to do: Show the children the poster of the skeleton and discuss with them which bones correspond with their arms, legs, chest etc. Name the bones for them.

Using the resources listed above, encourage the children to draw and cut bones out of card to make a skeleton. Lay the cut-out bones on a table and help the children identify if anything vital is missing. Support the children in putting the skeleton together, using the stapler (closely supervised) and / or sticky tape. Use the crocodile clips to join the arms and legs to the main torso. This will enable the arms and legs to move and dangle once the skeleton is hung up.

To make the hands ask each child to draw around their own hand on card (with fingers spread out wide). Show how to make a fold at each finger and thumb joint, then cut short lengths of craft straws and secure these to each digit. Fingers will need three pieces of straw and thumbs just two.

Thread string through each finger, securing it firmly at the finger tips, and more loosely at the 'wrist'. Pull the strings and watch the hand make a grasping action.

Read *Funnybones* stories with the children and sing 'Them bones, them bones'.

Energy food for Teddy

Learning opportunity: Understanding the importance of eating healthily

Early Learning Goal: Physical Development. Children will learn about the importance of keeping healthy.

Resources: A teddy, a white board, a large sheet of card, pens and pencils, marker pens, a ruler, a selection of food packaging or pictures of food from magazines, advertising material etc. A visual image showing the main food groups (proteins, carbohydrates, dairy products, vitamins and minerals, and fats and oils.)

Key vocabulary: Names of healthy foods, particularly those that give us energy (bread, pasta, rice cereals etc.)

Organisation: A whole group activity.

What to do: Encourage the children to reflect back on earlier discussions and display work on healthy and not-so-healthy foods. Draw their attention to the food groups and ask them what they remember about each group.

Explain that Teddy needs help in knowing what he should eat to give him energy and keep him healthy, especially on the days he plays football (e.g. Saturday mornings) and does athletics (e.g. Wednesdays afternoons).

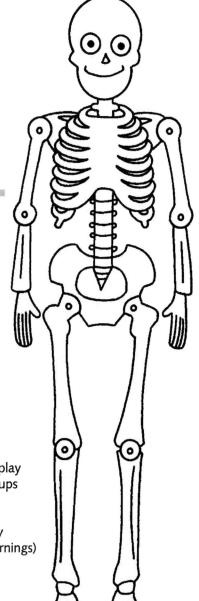

Help the children draw up a weekly menu for Teddy, writing their ideas for them initially onto a whiteboard, then making changes as they develop their ideas about his food and nutritional needs. Remember to link Teddy's needs to their own energy needs, especially when they have been physically active.

When everyone is happy with Teddy's menu, display it for everyone to see.

Display: Set up a sequenced (storyboard style) wall display, divided into four main sections from left to right. Starting on the left, display the children's skeletons, next display images of body organs with appropriate labels attached. The third section will ideally include a display of healthy foods, and the final section of the display will be photos of sportsmen and women 'in action' and, if you have them, photos of the children playing sport or being physically active.

Encouraging Early Sports Skills

Week 2 Ball skills

Personal, Social and Emotional development

■ During circle time talk about ball sports. Who can think of sports that involve the use of a ball? Who has been to a game or match? Who watches sport on television and who do they watch it with? Which sports do they enjoy watching best and what do they like about them? (PS4)

■ Take all opportunities to help children identify when they are working as part of a team. Ask them to think about which sports are played as teams and what being part of a team means. (PS8)

■ Provide freely available activities that encourage the fine motor skills needed for throwing and catching, and the dexterity and hand-eye coordination needed for aiming in planned directions. Include balls, quoits, hoops and beanbags as well as activities such as jigsaws, construction, dressing and undressing dolls, dressing-up clothes with a range of fastenings, dough and clay for moulding, threading activities and of course writing, drawing and mark making. (PS12)

Communication, Language and Literacy

■ Introduce the children to the vocabulary linked specifically to the shape of a ball and to ball sports. Introduce words such as bounce, goal, score, pass, kick, hit, bowl, spin, as well as round, sphere, globe etc. Read stories about ball sports. See pages 58-59 for a list of suggested titles. (L5)

■ Provide sheets of card and bold marker pens for children to make signs to either a) hold up during sports games when they are the spectators e.g. the name of their favourite sports team, the word 'Goal' or 'Score', or b) that can then be used during an exercise session, encouraging healthy exercise whilst at the same time helping letter and word recognition e.g. 'run, jump, skip, throw' etc. (L18)

■ Help the children to sort a range of sports kit and equipment by size, colour, weight etc. Set it out on a display table and provide relevant resources in order for them to label it. (L19)

Problem Solving, Reasoning and Numeracy

■ As a class or group, collect a range of balls in different sizes, colours and materials. Help the children to sort and classify them by size order or by a particular function. Use large hoops to provide easy sorting areas and with slightly older children overlap the hoops in a Venn diagram style to show how an object can be part of more than one group e.g. a blue football can be classified with other large balls, or with other blue balls. (N13)
■ Use measuring sticks to measure out pre-determined sizes of sports areas such as a pitch for playing football or a court for playing tennis. Encourage children to predict how many 'stick lengths', 'how many more' etc. Cricket bats, tennis rackets etc could be used instead of measuring sticks. Provide playground chalk for the markings. (N5)
■ Show the children a traditionally sewn football made from hexagonal shapes. Count the sides of the hexagons together and also count up how many hexagons were needed to make the football (eighteen). Provide the children with ready-cut hexagon shapes, or marked out shapes for them to cut out themselves. Encourage them to tessellate and make patterns. Count out eighteen hexagons together (using a pattern size from the traditional football shown to the children earlier), and try sticking them to a real football to see if they can cover it completely without any gaps. (N10)

Knowledge and Understanding of the World

■ Discuss with the children sports events that are currently topical e.g. the Olympic Games, World Athletics Championships, Football World Cup, Rugby World Cup, Wimbledon Tennis Championships, the FA Cup Final etc and help them find the relevant places or countries on a globe or large map. (K9)
■ Using 'junk' or another modelling medium, make models of famous sports buildings and places e.g. Wembley Stadium, the Centre Court at Wimbledon. Alternatively paint pictures of them instead. Provide visual images for children who have never seen them before, and as prompts for those who require them. (K5)
■ Provide a range of balls of differing textures e.g. rubber, foam, plastic, wood, padded material (e.g. a baby toy), woolly pom-poms etc. Encourage each child to bounce, throw and catch each type of ball several times. Discuss as a group how they differ and which balls are easiest to bounce, to throw and to catch. Encourage the children to explore their ideas and ask questions to find out why. (K4)

Physical Development

■ Focus physical play on ball skills, both indoors and outdoors. Practice throwing and catching, using balls of different sizes. Set up both paired and group activities according to each pair or group's skill and individual ball confidence. Set up specific ball games such as netball, basketball or dodgeball when you think the children are ready. (PD7)
■ Make number lines for each sport you discuss with the children e.g. two children line up to indicate tennis, five children for basketball, eleven children for football. (PD2)

Creative Development

■ Make a display with the children using sports kit and equipment. This could be team focused e.g. Manchester United or Chelsea football teams, colour focused e.g. any team that wears blue, or sport focused e.g. items associated with tennis such as clothes, rackets, ball, netting, trophies, strawberries and cream etc. (C2)

- Make footballs from papier-mâché using balloons, paper and paste. See activity on page 42. (C3)
- Provide round items for children to paint and decorate as 'balls'. (C5)

Catch and throw activity

Learning opportunity: Learning to catch and throw a ball

Early Learning Goal: Physical Development. Children will be learning to use a range of small equipment and how to move with control and coordination. They will also be learning awareness of space, of themselves and of others.

Resources: Balls of various sizes and textures, beanbags and quoits. Large hoops, buckets, baskets or sturdy boxes will also be useful. If you have a netball or basketball hoop, that will be helpful too.

Key vocabulary: Words associated with catching and throwing e.g. aim, direction, position, grasp, underarm, overarm, one-handed, two-handed etc.

Organisation: This can easily be a whole group activity providing there is sufficient space for all children to move around safely.

What to do: Get everyone 'warmed up' by each child selecting a resource (ball, quoit or beanbag), and giving them time to practice handling it and throwing it up and catching it again. Next, encourage the children to explore what else they can do with it e.g. throw it high and catch it, throw it forward and run to catch it. Can it bounce? etc.

Set the hoops, buckets, baskets or boxes at one end of the room or play area and encourage the children to run towards them and throw their resource in. Set a chalk line for them to stay behind when they throw. Gradually move the line further away. Let them try this with each type of resource. Which do they find easiest to get in the hoops? Encourage them to think why this is (e.g. balls may bounce out again, quoits are hard to aim and may go in a very different direction to the one they intended if not held correctly to start with, whereas beanbags stay where they land.) Demonstate throwing techniques for children who are struggling.

If you have netball or basketball hoops, set them up.

Once the children have explored throwing and catching each resource, remove all resources except the balls. Set up a four point circuit in which the children need to a) bounce their ball in a hoop, b) throw it in the air and catch it, c) run to a hoop and score a goal / basket, and then d) throw the ball into a box or bucket. Let them repeat the circuit as many times as time allows, using balls of different sizes if possible.

End the session with the children sitting quietly in pairs, gently throwing small balls or beanbags to each other as a 'warm down' activity.

Making footballs

Learning opportunity: Making footballs using papier-mâché.

Early Learning Goal: Creative Development. Children will be exploring texture, shape and form in three dimensions.

Resources: Lots of old newspapers, wallpaper paste (a non-fungal variety), water, buckets, balloons.

Key vocabulary: Words linked to ball shapes e.g. round, sphere, globe, and words to describe the experience of making papier-mâché e.g. sticky, slimy, mushy, gunky.

Organisation: In small groups of four to six with a supervising adult.

What to do: At the beginning of the week explain to the children what papier-mâché is and that it takes quite a long time to dry out. Provide blown-up balloons for each child (approximately football sized), as the frame for their football. Do not allow children to blow up their own balloons as some young children tend to suck in between blows, risking sucking the balloon into the mouths and choking.

As a group tear up the newspapers into narrow strips, and then help the children to measure out the appropriate ratio of powder paste to water in a bucket. Let the children mix it thoroughly using a long-handled paintbrush.

Model for the children how to soak the newspaper strips in the paste and then gradually cover their balloon with soggy newspaper. They will need several layers all over the balloon in order to end up with a firm 'football'. You may need to assist younger children in achieving this.

Leave the 'footballs' somewhere warm to dry out. Once they are completely dry let the children choose whether they want to either paint or decorate their balls.

Display: Display balls however you can e.g. by size, by texture, by colour. Use large hoops to show how some balls can be grouped by more than one feature (using the Venn diagram pattern). Edge the wall display with the printed 'ball' pictures the children have made and hang the papier-mâché footballs in a large net from the ceiling or a high hook.

Week 3 Balance and coordination

Personal, Social and Emotional development

- During circle time ask children to think about times when they need to use balance e.g. when standing on tip-toes, reaching up high for something, during certain games etc. Encourage them to think what might happen if they were unable to balance, and what parts of the body they are using to keep themselves steady. Explain to them how the inner ear also helps with balance, and that this is why they can feel dizzy if they spin around too quickly or too much. (PS3)
- During a physical play session encourage children to work in pairs to support each other in trying to balance on one leg and also to walk carefully along a bench or chalk line without 'falling off'. You may find it helpful initially to match each pair evenly both in size and in temperament. (PS7)
- If possible, invite local people to demonstrate activities that involve balance and co-ordination e.g. Yoga, Tai Chi, general keep fit etc. Encourage children to try the activities alongside the visitors. (PS1)

Communication, Language and Literacy

- Introduce vocabulary relevant to balance and co-ordination. Include terms such as stable, tilt, lean, concentrate, level, vertical, horizontal, poise, positioning, equalize, self-control, strength. (L5)
- Play a game such as 'Simon says' where 'Simon' gives instructions linked to balance e.g. lean to your left, stand on one leg, bend forward and touch your toes etc (L3)
- In small groups play the floor game 'Twister' where children have to place either a hand or a foot onto an area of a specific colour. How hard is it for them to keep balanced? Following playing the game, ask the children to describe what they did to try to keep balanced. Help them reflect on how the game becomes more difficult with more people playing. (L7)

Problem Solving, Reasoning and Numeracy

- Explore the principles of balance through a variety of construction activities, using both commercial and natural resources. Discuss with the children why some buildings are standing more securely than others. You may need to deliberately make some examples yourself if a range of stable and unstable constructions do not naturally materialise during the activity. Link the principles of balance during construction play to balance within the body. (N4)
- Introduce the children to games such as 'Jenga' where they have to take blocks away, trying not to let the building fall. Encourage the children to predict and reflect on when, why and what made it fall and describe the position of the piece they are removing e.g. it is under the red block, next to a brown block, but on top of a white block etc. (N12)

Knowledge and Understanding of the World

- Provide scales and containers, together with a range of natural materials for children to measure out and explore issues of balance and the need for equal weights on both sides of the centre of something. Relate these experiments to the balance they needed during physical activities they enjoyed previously. (K3)

■ Show the children a recording of gymnasts performing then, if possible, take them to visit a real gymnastics setting. Let them see at first hand the narrowness of the beams and bars that gymnasts manoeuvre around so easily. Provide a beam or bar at floor level for them to move across. Encourage them to talk about how easy or difficult they find it. If possible, arrange for them to enjoy a movement session on the mats used by floor gymnasts. (K10)

■ Explore the animal world with the children and look at the different ways in which animals move and balance. What have they observed? E.g. who uses two feet? Who uses four? Who uses their tails (prehensile use)? Which animals are the best at balancing? Why might this be? During a physical session let the children pretend to be a range of animals, moving and balancing as accurately as they can. Make links back to the movements of gymnasts and other sports people. (K9)

Physical Development

■ Set up a low level obstacle course for the children to move around. Help them to decide initially what should be included, giving them clear explanations as to why anything unsuitable they suggested cannot be used. Agree in advance how they should move e.g. on their feet, on their hands and knees etc. See the activity opposite. (PD1)

■ Position carpet squares a little way apart from each other either in lines or in zig-zag shapes. Who can get across them all without touching the floor? (PD 3)

■ Teach the children how to play games that involve co-ordination and balance such as 'Hopscotch' and 'musical statues' etc. (PD4)

Creative Development

■ Set up a weaving activity using fine string or wool together with strips of card fastened into a circle. Help the children to make a 'tennis racket'. Once the weaving is complete, fasten off securely and provide suitable resources for them to add a 'handle' of their own choice to their racket. Display the rackets and follow this up with racket play outside. (C5)

■ Talk about, and if possible listen to, a range of sports tunes, songs and chants. As a group let the children decide what they would like to 'compose' something for. E.g. it could be in readiness for the family sports day at the end of the topic. Involve musical instruments and singing, practicing regularly together. Make a recording of the chant or song when you feel the children are ready. Encourage them to reflect on the recording. Can they hear themselves? Can they identify any pattern or repetition in the recording? What else can they identify? How would they describe the recording to others? (C4)

■ Encourage the children to paint pictures of different types of people using balancing skills e.g. gymnasts, sportsmen and women, clowns, circus performers. (C5)

Moving around

Learning opportunity: Learning to keep balanced whilst negotiating an obstacle course.

Early Learning Goal: Physical Development. Children will be learning to move with confidence, imagination and in safety. They will also be moving with control and coordination.

Resources: Low benches, impact-absorbent mats, trampette, hoops, carpet squares, a low A-frame.

Key vocabulary: Balance, hold, still, steady, careful, precise, dismount, concentrate, control, level, self-control.

Organisation: As a whole group, providing there is sufficient space and equipment for children to move safely.

What to do: Set out the resources suitable for the layout of your setting. For the warm up: encourage the children to jog gently on the spot.

Sit the children down to watch while you model the actions you want them to include in their obstacle course. Obstacles can include: a) walk along a bench with arms held out sideways, b) make two star jumps (or forward rolls) across a large mat, c) bounce three times on the trampette with a dismount onto a mat, d) step in and out of the hoops (positioned in two rows) as fast as you can, one foot to each hoop, e) climb over the A-frame, f) hop from carpet square to carpet square and then finally sit down on a large mat to rest and observe the other children. To warm down: jog gently on the spot again and then sit ready to go and get changed or move to other activities.

The Sports and Leisure Centre

Learning opportunity: Using prior knowledge and experience during role-play to show understanding of what happens in a sports and leisure centre.

Early Learning Goal: Creative Development. Children will be using their imagination in role play.

Resources: Exercise mats, a large impact-absorbent mat, towels, swimming hats, goggles, a bench for balancing, a trampette, rackets and shuttlecocks (balls will not be suitable in such an unsupervised environment), leotards and 'jogging' suits, resources for buying and selling entrance tickets, and items for a café (cups, plates etc).

Key vocabulary: Names of activities e.g. swimming, gymnastics, badminton, Tai Chi, Yoga, keep fit etc.

Organisation: Small groups, using the usual setting guidance regarding numbers of children able to use the role-play area at any one time.

What to do: Help the children to turn the role play area into a sports and leisure centre, supporting them in writing signs and making tickets, and scribing for them as needed. Decide together what 'activities' will be available at the sports and leisure centre and gather together suitable equipment and resources. Supervise from afar, allowing the children the freedom to explore ideas and their imagination.

Display: Make a display about balance and co-ordination. Use construction models made by the children, and also the 'Jenga' game, adding appropriate labels to highlight the relevant vocabulary. Also, display the woven tennis rackets. On the wall, display the children's pictures of people balancing, and if you have taken photographs of the children, add these to the display.

If space allows, provide a set of balance scales and a range of different objects to be weighed, enabling the children to consolidate their understanding of weight and balance.

Week 4 Creative bodies

Personal, Social and Emotional development

- Collect together a selection of photographs of sports people showing a range of different expressions e.g. delight, despair, anger, confusion, astonishment etc. Ask the children to decide what each person was feeling at the time and what might have happened to cause the expression. If you know the real answer and think the children will understand it then explain it to them. Can they make the same expression? Provide children with mirrors and encourage them to use a variety of expressions, body actions and gestures. Let them pair up with a friend and then observe and copy each other's actions. Which do they consider to be positive expressions and which are negative expressions? Discuss why. (PS2)
- Use pictures of emotions as a basis for discussion of emotion and the expressions that can indicate each emotion. Encourage the children to think how their expressions, gestures and actions can impact on how other people think about them, approach them and react to them, and also how other people's expressions or actions might mean they are in need of friendship and someone to talk to. (PS5)
- Play a game in which you give children clues as to what sport you are playing. Initially describe the various body movements involved, then add in further details such as numbers of players, what equipment they use, what clothes they usually wear etc. How many clues do the group need before they guess? (PS1)

Communication, Language and Literacy

- Read stories such as *Angelina Ballerina* and talk about the actions Angelina and the other mice make as they dance. Ask who has ever been dancing and encourage those children to talk about their dancing classes or experiences. If practical, ask children to demonstrate dancing steps or positions and name them for the others in the class or group. (L3)
- Introduce children to vocabulary linked to creative movement and expression. Include terms such as flow, glide, float, hover, twirl, swoop, posture, pirouette, sequence, active, still. Practice these 'actions' during a movement session. (L5)

Problem Solving, Reasoning and Numeracy

- In groups make a number line of gymnasts by providing materials for the children to draw, cut out and 'dress' people performing. Encourage them to also write the numbers from one to (a maximum of) ten, one number to be placed on the clothes of each performer. If appropriate provide a number line for the children to use as a reminder of how to write each number. Let each group of children sort their gymnasts out into the correct numerical order and display them on a wall. (N1)
- Plan a simple gymnastics routine together using a range of movements and directions. Help the children to remember the sequence of the routine by calling out the direction they should be moving in. Let confident children have a go at taking the place of 'leader' of the routine. (N12)
- Give each child a number to remember, from 1 to 9. Ensure they are familiar with the number you have given them. Play beautiful music and encourage them to dance and move freely in a large circle according to how the music makes them feel. From time to time, gain their attention, for example by clapping your hands, or rattling a tambourine,

and hold up a number. The children who had previously been given that number now dance in the middle of the circle. Repeat the game, ensuring that all numbers have been called out and all children have danced within the centre of the circle. (N3)

Knowledge and Understanding of the World

■ Watch a short DVD of a ballet. Encourage the children to use their observations of the DVD in their own dance movements. Use the experience as a discussion point, linking it to the movements also used by both beam and floor gymnasts. (K2)

■ Invite as many different dancers to visit your setting as you can, or if this is not possible, gather media footage of different types of dancing. Ideally try to provide demonstrations of ballet dancing, tap dancing, ballroom dancing, disco dancing and break dancing. Help the children to explore the similarities between the dancers, and how the different types of dancers do things differently. E.g. how were they using their bodies differently? Make links to health and fitness and also to balance and coordination. Which type of dancing did the children enjoy watching best? (K3)

■ Provide a range of hoops, ribbons and batons for the children to use and let them practice twirling them. These skills are not easy, so encourage the children to ask questions about techniques and why some techniques are successful and others less successful. Try and demonstrate appropriate techniques for them yourself. See activity opposite. (K4)

Physical Development

■ Again, using lengths of ribbon to swirl, twirl and generally 'express themselves' with, encourage the children to move creatively around the room without bumping into others. (PD4)

■ During a movement session, explain to the children that they are going to be imaginary sportsmen and women. Give them a range of sports which they have to demonstrate e.g. when you say 'cricket' they may become a bowler, or stand-ready with their

Key vocabulary: Words linked to the fine physical actions involved in making the pom-poms e.g. wind, thread, loop, weave, pull, overlap, etc., as well as the physical gestures used in cheerleading e.g. march, dance, perform, shake, wave, wiggle, star jump.

Organisation: Making the pom-poms takes quite a long time, so ideally, set up the activity each day and encourage children to join in the activity for a short while on several occasions. Pom-poms could be made as a group which would take less time. Assuming you will have five or six cheerleaders 'performing' at any one time, you will therefore need to make ten or twelve pom-poms.

What to do: Model for the children how to draw round the circle shapes. The small circle needs to be in the centre of the larger one. Each large circle needs its middle cut out, leaving a cardboard ring. Each pom-pom is made from two cardboard rings.

For each pom-pom, tie one end of a small (softly-wound) ball of wool around the two cardboard circles. The children then need to wind the wool round and round the cardboard circle gradually covering it all over. This continues until it becomes too difficult to thread anymore wool through the central hole.

Using sharp scissors, an adult will need to cut through the wool, and between the two cardboard rings, without letting the wool slip, all the way round. Once all the wool has been cut through, a length of strong wool must be tied tightly between the cardboard circles, securing the wool into a pom-pom. The cardboard circles can now be cut and removed. The pom-pom is ready to use by the cheerleaders.

Help the children develop a simple routine, taking it in turns to accompany sports activities.

Display: Make a display together of as many creative resources used in sport and gymnastics as you can e.g. ribbons, batons, hoops, pom-poms. If you can, acquire a national flag to use as a base cloth for the display, or paint Olympic rings onto old white sheeting material. Pin photos of sports men and women, gymnasts and athletes on a board, each demonstrating how they move creatively within their sport or event. Agree a description of how they move with the children, and write down captions for each photo. Hang the pom-poms on the display when they are not in use.

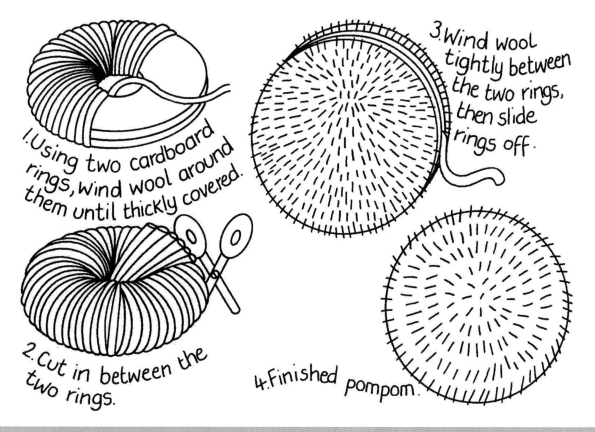

1. Using two cardboard rings, wind wool around them until thickly covered.

2. Cut in between the two rings.

3. Wind wool tightly between the two rings, then slide rings off.

4. Finished pompom.

Week 5 Space, direction and orientation

Personal, Social and Emotional Development

- Talk to the children about how sports people need to be able to run, kick the ball etc. whilst always being aware of other players, and team members, and where they are at any time. Ask them to tell you why this is important and what might happen if they do not have this kind of awareness. Link this discussion to themselves playing outside. How important is this to the children as they play? Remind the children of the setting's rules regarding running etc. and link back to the notion of rules in various sports. (PS9)
- Sports people use their sense of direction all the time. In ball sports they need to kick or hit balls towards specific goals, over nets, towards specific spots etc. For athletes, when they jump they need to land in certain areas, when they run they need to keep within the boundaries of their lanes, and as they throw javelins and shotputs they need to stay within safety margins, away from spectators. Help children practice using their sense of direction and keeping within margins by setting up a range of targets for them to kick a ball against, throw a beanbag at, jump onto, over or in between. Discuss with them why keeping to boundaries is important. (PS10)

Communication, Language and Literacy

- Introduce vocabulary linked to direction. Include terms such as forward, backward, left, right, sideways, across, between, over, under, next to, beside, around, along. (L5)
- Provide resources for children to make arrow signs and set up a display together, adding captions to label each direction. Encourage each child to draw a 'plan' of arrows on a sheet of paper. In pairs let them consolidate their understanding of direction by giving each other directions to follow, moving a small toy around the arrows they have drawn e.g. two to the left, one going forwards, one to the right etc. Who can follow the instructions and end up in the right place? (L19)

Problem Solving, Reasoning and Numeracy

- Play rolling games using marbles or small balls, using a flat surface marked out into 'lanes'. Give the children time to practice so they can try and find out how speed, height from the ground etc. affects the direction they are aiming for. Who can keep their marble or ball in the right lane? If using marbles, children must be carefully supervised at all times. With very young children golf, table-tennis or squash balls will be a safer option as they are less likely to be a choking hazard. (N4)
- Make video recordings of the children racing against each other and playing various sports. Watch the recordings with a few children at a time in several small groups, encouraging the children to take turns in describing what is happening, using vocabulary to describe the positions of the runners or players. Have any issues regarding space, or direction been observed? (N12)
- Set up games such as skittles or boules and let children practice directing balls in specific directions. (N4)

Knowledge and Understanding of the World

- Provide programmable toys for the children either in pairs or small groups. Help them master the skill of directed movement and then encourage each pair or group to follow a simple set of instructions you have prepared in advance. Once the children are confident with the activity, let them plan their own route and then try to follow it. This route can be drawn by the children, who will then follow the lines of their own drawings e.g. left, right, straight on, go back, or written down and read to them by either an adult or a more confident reader. (K7)
- Challenge the children to make a race track for a group of small teddies to have a race (30cm size teddies would be ideal). What resources will they need? What size will the race track need to be and how wide will the running lanes be? Support their ideas and thinking and provide opportunities that will encourage prediction, reflection and questions. Enjoy racing the teddies when the track is ready, and follow this up with other races, e.g. racing small cars, always aiming to keep them in their initial lanes. (K5)

Physical Development

- Set up paired sports games such as tennis. Initially let the children practice gaining control of the racket, and then encourage them to start hitting the ball to and fro between themselves. Who can keep sending the ball in the right direction? As each pair's skills increase introduce a 'net'. This could be a length of net curtain fastened to two posts or chairs, or even a skipping rope. Can they keep the ball higher than the net? From time to time change the pairings of the children. Use your observations of their developing skills to pair more able children together, helping them each to develop their skills further. (PD2)
- Provide opportunities for children to have complete freedom of choice when using a range of sports equipment and resources. Can they develop their own ideas for a new 'sport'? Remind them of the need to be aware of others as they play, observing where others are positioned and thinking about how much space they need or are going to need. (PD4)
- Provide thick chalk or masking tape lines for children to try to walk along without going 'off the edge'. Teach the children to take 'pigeon steps', one foot positioned in front of the other, heel to toe, heel to toe. (PD2)

Creative Development

- Provide media footage of a synchronised sport of some kind e.g. team gymnastics, or synchronised diving. Talk initially with the children about how each gymnast is doing the same action but coming from a different direction. Explore with them what they would need to consider e.g. timing, careful observation, plenty of practice. Follow this up by teaching the children simple country dancing sequences, where they need to form lines, dance in pairs, move to the centre of a square of four people etc. Let them hold ribbons in one hand and enjoy how they move and twirl as they dance with their partners. (C5)
- During a movement session, encourage the children to move creatively (glide, fly, float, twirl etc.) in the direction you call out to them. Change the direction regularly, but not too quickly. Children need time to adjust to a new direction, and calling out changes too quickly is likely to cause collisions. (C5)
- Encourage children to draw or paint pictures of sports with specific boundaries e.g. running races, hurdling, tennis matches etc. (C5)

Avoiding the balls

Learning opportunity: Understanding direction and orientation by avoiding being touched by balls rolled towards them, leading on to a game of 'dodgeball'.

Early Learning Goal: Physical Development. Children will be showing their developing awareness of space, of themselves and of others.

Resources: Large balls and plenty of space.

Key vocabulary: Words linked to actions that help them avoid being touched by the balls e.g. jump over, between, sideways, star jumps, leaps, space, direction.

Organisation: Can be as a large group, ideally with several adults rolling the balls from different positions.

What to do: Model for younger children different ways of getting over a ball without it touching them and ask them to think of any other ideas they could try. Remind them that many sports need quick reactions. Make a specific mention of the need to avoid balls during the game 'dodgeball', which they will be playing later on.

Warm up by encouraging the children to jump from side to side, and backwards and forwards.

Adults start to roll (not throw) the balls towards the children who do their best not to be touched by the ball, and also to avoid bumping into other people. Encourage them to jump, run, dodge and leap.

If time and space allows, set up short 'dodgeball' games with groups of children. Remember that only soft sponge balls must be used.

Warm down by using gentle stretches to ease bodies, and calm excited minds.

Maypole movements

Learning opportunity: Developing an understanding of space and direction as they move in and out of each other during the maypole dance.

Early Learning Goal: Personal, Social and Emotional Development. Children will be working as part of a group, taking turns and understanding that there needs to be agreed codes of behaviour for groups of people to work together harmoniously.

Resources: A tall pole held securely in position (a washing post or tree outside can work well). Also, long lengths of ribbon tied to a disk at the top of the pole. The most traditional colours are yellow, white and green. Florist's ribbon can work very well for this (approximately 5-6 cms wide). Also, a CD player and some 'country dance' type music.

Key vocabulary: Dance, follow, lead, turn, left, right, twist, plait, round.

Organisation: Groups of ten or twelve children will be ideal, but you could set up a maypole dance with as few as six or as many as sixteen.

What to do: Although not technically a 'sport', this activity is a lovely summer term event that will contribute to children's development of skills needed to enjoy and play sport, as they will be working co-operatively, moving in time with each other and developing their orientation and spatial awareness.

Explain to the children what a maypole is and the importance of the maypole dancers needing to understand space and direction and where they are in relation to the other dancers to avoid colliding during the routine.

In advance, tie the ribbons to either a) a disk at the top of the maypole to allow the ribbons to move round with the children (this is recommended when working with very

imaginary bat. When you say 'basketball' they may start jumping up high to try to score an imaginary 'basket'. (PD1)

Creative Development

■ Invite a group of cheerleaders from the local university to come and demonstrate their routines for the children. Encourage them to teach the children a simple routine that they can practice together and perform at a later date, e.g. the family sports day at the end of the topic. (C4)
■ Make pom-poms with the children to use during their cheerleading routines. See activity opposite. (C3)
■ Dividing the group into two halves, and providing a range of musical instruments, each half of the group takes turns to play music for the other half to move to. (C1)

Floor routines

Learning opportunity: Putting physical actions into a routine.

Early Learning Goal: Physical Development. Children will move with confidence and in safety. They will move with control and co-ordination and show awareness of space, of themselves, and of others.

Resources: A large clear floor space with impact-absorbent mats spread around.

Key vocabulary: Names of physical actions e.g. run, jump, roll, stretch, leap, skip, march, twirl, perform.

Organisation: As a whole group, or working in small groups.

What to do: Warm up by encouraging the children to bend and stretch gently. Explain the actions you want the children to practice. This could include a) touching their toes, b) stretching arms up high whilst on tiptoes, c) star jumps, d) running a short distance and ending with a leap, e) forwards and or backward rolls, and f) actions such as skipping, marching and twirling.

You will probably only include four actions initially, building on this as children grow in confidence. Encourage the children to work in small groups, and from time to time, to sit and watch each other and celebrate each others performances.

Develop a short routine using ribbons for the sports day event.

Warm down by encouraging gentle bends and stretches, and running on the spot to end the session.

Making pom-poms

Learning opportunity: Making pom-poms and being cheerleaders

Early Learning Goal: Creative Development. Children will be exploring colour, texture, shape and form in two and three dimensions.

Resources: Cardboard (breakfast cereal packets will be ideal), scissors, plenty of wool, and two different sized circle shapes to draw around, approximately 12cm and 3.5cm wide (a saucer and a camera film pot will be ideal).

young children), or b) to a fixed point at the top of a pole which will enable the ribbons to be twisted and braided as children move in and out of each other.

Play music to give both rhythm and the impetus to dance. Model for the children what they need to do e.g. they can all skip together, and simply concentrate on moving in the same direction and keeping the same pace and distance between themselves and the dancers on either side of them. From time to time change the direction they are dancing in.

Older children can be taught simple movements which allow the ribbons to braid in the traditional manner. Instructions for these movements can be found on the various internet search engines.

Display: Using yellow, white and green ribbons, help the children to make a maypole picture for the wall. In between the ribbon of the picture, position their paintings of sports people, athletes and gymnasts. Support the children in writing captions for the display, scribing for them as needed.

Week 6 Teamwork and co-operation

Personal, Social and Emotional development

- Talk with the children about rules and boundaries. What do these terms mean to them? What rules and boundaries can they think of at home? In the early years setting? Discuss why each is important and make the link to team situations and share ideas as to why they are especially important when working or playing with others. (PS9)
- Encourage the children to describe what sort of people they like playing or working with. Decide as a group what each of their suggestions means and get them to explain why that particular attribute in a person is good to have within a team. (PS10)

Communication, Language and Literacy

- Introduce and discuss terms linked to working with others. Include terms such as help, assist, working together, joint effort, helpfulness, respond, squad etc. (L5)
- During circle time talk about a team sport event that is currently topical and that most children will know something about. Support the children in describing the sporting event, where it takes place, how it is set out and whatever information they can think of linked to the players, the resources and the process. Draw their attention to how the team members work together in order to score, win etc. Help them to reflect on when they have worked with others towards a joint aim. This could be during physical activity or any other aspect of the time at the setting, or they may have examples from home, working with siblings or friends. (L8)
- Play a 'sporting' version of the game I went to the market and I bought … e.g. start off by saying 'I went to watch the athletics and first of all I saw…' Encourage each child in turn to repeat what you have said and add another athletics event that they have seen. With younger children it will be helpful to have visual images displayed nearby to help them. This game can also be used to tell the process of a sports match or game, each child adding another 'action'. (L6)

Problem Solving, Reasoning and Numeracy

- In small groups design and make a football pitch together, using a range of paper shapes e.g. rectangles, squares, circle, semi-circles etc. Support the children in preparing the shapes and in cutting them out. Provide a visual image to get them started and for them to refer to as they work. Link this to the suggestion for Knowledge and Understanding of the World activity too. Encourage the use of relevant vocabulary to describe both shape and size, and remind them of the correct names of each area of the pitch. (N11)

Knowledge and Understanding of the World

- Linking to the suggestion for Problem Solving, Reasoning and Numeracy, support the children in developing football pitches together in groups, using a range of paper or cardboard shapes e.g. rectangles, squares, circle, semi-circles etc. Support the children in selecting the materials, and preparing the shapes and in cutting them out. Provide a range of appropriate resources for them to secure and assemble each football pitch. (K6)

■ Gather together an array of medals, trophies and certificates for the children to look at, handle, admire and discuss. Some children may already have a certificate or badge for swimming or dancing or early gymnastics. Encourage these children to bring them in and tell everyone about what they needed to do to gain them. Find out what the staff and parents have achieved as well. Again, encourage them to come and share their stories with the children. If you have local sports teams, enquire whether they have a trophy they could bring in or lend you. Explain to the children how teams often display their trophies in a glass cabinet and follow this up by making trophies and medals, and drawing or printing certificates together. Use these for the sports day celebrations with parents and friends. (K5)

Physical Development

■ Set up relay races in small teams of four or six. Encourage each team to pick a team leader and to decide between themselves what order they will take part in. (PD 6)

Creative Development

■ Let the children pair themselves up and take it in turns to choose an action or a movement to demonstrate to their partner. The children need to carefully watch each other's movements and then copy the action as best as they can. If possible, provide large mirrors for them to observe both themselves and their partner. (C1)

Sports day races

Learning opportunity: Learning about racing, both individual and relay.

Early Learning Goal: Personal, Social and Emotional Development. Children will be forming good relationships with their peers.

Resources: Hessian sacks, balls, baskets, large spoons plus hard-boiled eggs (or something similar), hoops, beanbags. A camera to take photographs.

Key vocabulary: Words associated with racing e.g. run, jump, win, relay, team effort, co-operate, succeed, taking turns.

Organisation: A whole group activity with plenty of supervising adults to organise and monitor the events.

What to do: Decide in advance what races you will include and gather appropriate resources to support them. Include at least two different relay team events.

Ensure that there is a clear racing area. You may find it helpful to mark it out roughly with playground chalk.

Divide the children into teams for relay events. Relay events could involve the child running to a hoop, dropping in a bean bag and running back again as fast as they can so that the next member of their team can run. An alternative would be throwing a ball into a box, pulling a large hoop over their head etc. but always running back to where they started. If you have plenty of space, a relay event involving the traditional four team member approach could be set up, positioning the team members at various points around the outside of the play area with each runner handing a 'baton' onto the next runner as they reach them. Young children may find it easier to hand over something like a teddy, as they can grasp it more easily.

Enjoy egg and spoon races, jumping in sacks races etc. Give emphasis to enjoyment and taking part, rather than winning and losing.

Medals and Trophies

Learning opportunity: Making medals and trophies, and designing certificates to celebrate achievement at the family sports day event.

Early Learning Goal: Creative Development.Children will be expressing and communicating their ideas by using a range of materials and suitable tools to support their designing and making.

Resources: Scissors, A5 card (for making certificates), paper, sticky labels, pens, pencils, glue, sticky tape, stapler and staples, glitter, feathers, shiny paper and any craft items the setting has available.

Key vocabulary: Words and phrases linked to celebration e.g. medals, winners, achievers, good effort, well done, gold medal, silver medal, bronze medal. Also, words linked to creativity e.g. design, invent, create, construct, interesting, beautiful, unusual, unique, texture, two-dimensional, three-dimensional.

Organisation: In small groups with a supporting adult.

What to do: Remind the children of the medals, trophies and certificates they looked at and discussed earlier in the topic. Ask them to start thinking of ideas they could use to make some themselves. Show them the range of resources you have available for them to use.

Provide a template shape for a small trophy, for the children to use as a visual reminder of shape and size. Support children in drawing and cutting if needed.

Encourage the children to make a range of medals and trophies, and also provide A5 size sheets of card for them to design certificates. Scribe for them on the certificates as needed. It may be helpful to use large sticky labels (without the backing paper removed) as the base for medals. This will enable them to be attached easily to 'winners' at the family sports day event.

If you are able to get hold of an old (clean) fish tank, use it to display a trophy. Alternatively, use a cardboard box, with each side cut away, and cover it in clingfilm to imitate the glass. Again, display a trophy the children have made inside it.

Display: Use the photographs of the children taking part in the races as the main display, and add a variety of medals, trophies and certificates to show how achievement and taking part can be rewarded. This may be a good way of advertising the family sports day to parents and carers, using the parents' notice board for the display.

Bringing it all together

The ideal way to round off the 'Early Sports Skills' topic is to turn your setting into a sports stadium and hold a Sports Day. Invite parents to join you in a day/session of fun physical activities.

Preparation

- Decide which sports events you will include on the day and ensure that you have enough equipment for them all to take place simultaneously. You will also need to make sure you have enough staff (or parents) to organise, direct and supervise each 'event'.
- Arrange for photographs to be taken of each event.
- Prepare a brief opening ceremony with the children, perhaps with a small 'band' and a procession.
- Make a large sign to welcome parents and visitors to your sports event. You could perhaps use the five coloured rings image of the Olympic Games as its main feature.
- Have an adult supervise a small number of children as they hand out programmes.
- Set up a large board covered in paper shapes (balls of varying sizes, rackets, bats etc), and ask each person or family to add their names to a shape linked to their favourite sport.
- Decide on the direction you want everyone to move, and position large arrows to guide people. This will ensure that everyone sees or takes part in each event, and will help maintain a safer environment.

Activities

- Make printed bunting to decorate fences, the door etc., again using the colours of the Olympic rings.
- Mark out pitches, courts and race tracks in advance with the children. Include running races, simple relay races, jumping events, and gymnastic displays as well as some team games like short tennis, football and dodgeball. Encourage parents and children to watch and cheer the teams on.
- Provide mop heads for cheerleaders to dance with, or make large pom-poms with the children in advance, as in the activity in week 4.
- Cut out sports equipment 'shapes' for the visitors' board.
- Make medals and trophies as in the activity in week 6.

Food and drink

- Provide jugs of water and diluted fruit juice.
- Provide slices of orange (lemon will be too sour for most children) for children to suck during the 'half-time' match break. Ensure all pips have been carefully removed.

Recording the day

- Display a record of the topics covered over the past six weeks. This could be in a scrap book or on display boards. This would hopefully include photographs of the children taking part in each of the events and activities. Ensure each child is represented in some way.
- Provide opportunities for parents to add comments to the display, or have comment sheets available that can be collated and added later on.

Resources

Resources to collect

- Unwanted rolls of wallpaper or lining paper to use for 'high jump' activities.
- A whistle to start and stop matches and races.
- A loud hailer to gain everyone's attention
- Sacks (made from Hessian, not plastic) to use for races.
- Magazine and newspaper articles on sport for initiating discussion and as visual images.
- Sports memorabilia e.g. caps, shirts, scarves, programmes for discussion and display.
- Flipchart stands, pads of paper and chunky marker pens for scoreboards and team and event lists.
- Chalk boards and chalk, as flip charts.
- A stopwatch to help time races and events.

Everyday resources

- Clean plastic bottles with lids, washed and ready to be filled with sand or water and used as posts or markers.
- Sticky labels to label children or to use as 'medals', making it easy to attach these to the lucky winners.
- Old newspapers to use in the papier-mâché footballs activity.

Stories

There are a limited range of books available for young children linked to the topics of sport and fitness, but the following examples can be used to link to either the relevant sport, or to the themes of keeping fit, creative body use, balance and coordination. A few of the following titles were originally aimed at toddlers and a few at slightly older age ranges (5-7). All however can be successfully used with children across a broader age range. As with any new book, practitioners should familiarise themselves with the content and level of the books before reading them to a child or group of children to ensure suitability for the children's current stage in development and understanding. The following books were all available at the time of writing:

- *Goal!* by Colin McNaughton (Picture Lions)
- *Wonder Goal!* by Michael Foreman (Red Fox)
- *World Team* by Tim Vyner (Red Fox)
- *Stanley Bagshawe and the Short-sighted Football Trainer* by Bob Wilson (Barn Owl Books)
- *Football Fever* by Alan Durant and Kate Leake (MacMillan Children's Books)
- *Wicked Catch!* by Rob Childs and Michael Reid (Corgi Childrens)
- *Wicked Day!* by Rob Childs (Corgi Childrens)
- *Toddlerobics* by Zita Newcombe (Walker Books Ltd)
- *Toddlerobics: Animal Fun* by Zita Newcombe (Walker Books Ltd)
- *Pop-up Toddlerobics* by Zita Newcome (Walker Books Ltd)
- *Angelina and Alice* (Angelina Ballerina series) by Katharine Holabird and Helen Craig (Puffin Books)
- *Angelina on Stage* (Angelina Ballerina series) by Katharine Holabird and Helen Craig (Puffin Books)
- *Mrs Armitage and the Big Wave* by Quentin Blake (Red Fox)
- *Mrs Armitage on Wheels* by Quentin Blake (Red Fox)
- *Topsy and Tim in the Gym* by Jean Adamson, Gareth Adamson, and Nancy Hellen (Ladybird Books Ltd)

- *Topsy and Tim Learn to Swim* by Jean Adamson, Gareth Adamson, and Nancy Hellen (Ladybird Books Ltd)
- *Topsy and Tim go to the Park* by Jean Adamson, Gareth Adamson, and Nancy Hellen (Ladybird Books Ltd)
- *Topsy and Tim Ride their Bikes* by Jean and Gareth Anderson (E P Dutton)
- *Topsy and Tim at the Football Match* by Jean and Gareth Anderson (Dorling Kindersley Publishers Ltd)
- *Doing the Animal Bop* (Book and CD) by Jan Omerod and Lindsey Gardiner (Oxford University Press)
- *Whoosh Around the Mulberry Bush* (Book and CD) by Jan Omerod and Lindsey Gardiner (Oxford University Press)

Songs and rhymes

- *Head, shoulders, knees and toes* (this promotes co-ordinated body actions and the recognition of body parts).
- *Them bones, them bones* (this helps children to understand how their body fits together).
- National Anthems for the cultures represented in your group or class (or if this becomes too complex you could, as a whole group or class, choose a favourite tune to be your 'class' or 'group' anthem).
- *Five cheeky monkeys jumping on the bed* (plenty of jumping actions).
- *Five speckled frogs sitting on a speckled log* (again, plenty of jumping and hopping actions).
- *There was a princess long ago* (putting the emphasis on the actions of riding, galloping, weaving in and out etc).
- *This is the way we wash our hands* (linking this to exercise and health).

Books for adults

To support adults in their understanding of a range of sports and also the body and its workings, the following may be helpful:

- *The Sports Book: The Games – The Rules – The Tactics – The Techniques* (Dorling Kindersley)
- *Primary School Gymnastics* by Lawry Price (David Fulton Publishers Ltd)
- *Physical Education Key Stage 1* by Win Heath et al. (Nelson Thornes Ltd)
- *BTEC National Children's Care, Learning and Development Book 2, (Unit 12 - Physical activities for Children)* by Sandy Green, Sue Kellas, and Sally Foster (Nelson Thornes)
- *Human Form and Function* by Pamela Minett, David Wayne and David Rubenstein (Collins Educational)

Collecting evidence of children's learning

Monitoring children's development is an important task. Keeping a record of children's achievements will help you to see progress and will draw attention to those who are having difficulties for some reason. If a child needs additional professional help, such as speech therapy, your records will provide valuable evidence.

Records should be the result of collaboration between group leaders, parents and carers. Parents should be made aware of your record-keeping policies when their child joins your group. Show them the type of records you are keeping and make sure they understand that they have an opportunity to contribute. As a general rule, your records should form an open document. Any parent should have access to records relating to his or her child. Take regular opportunities to talk to parents about their children's progress. If you have formal discussions regarding children about whom you have particular concerns, a dated record of the main points should be kept.

Keeping it manageable

Records should be helpful in informing group leaders, appropriate adult helpers and parents and always be for the benefit of the child. However, keeping records of every aspect of each child's development can become a difficult task. The sample shown will help to keep records manageable and useful. The golden rule is to keep them simple.

Observations will basically fall into three categories:

■ Spontaneous records: Sometimes you will want to make a note of observations as they happen, for example a child is heard counting beanbags accurately during an activity, or is seen to play collaboratively for the first time.
■ Planned observations: Sometimes you will plan to make observations of children's developing skills in their everyday activities. Using the learning opportunity identified for an activity will help you to make appropriate judgements about children's capabilities and to record them systematically.

To collect information:

■ Talk to children about their activities and listen to their responses.
■ Listen to children talking to each other.
■ Observe children's work such as early writing, drawings, paintings and 3D models. (Keeping photocopies or photographs is sometimes useful.)

Sometimes you may wish to set up one-off activities for the purposes of monitoring development. Some groups, for example, ask children to make a drawing of themselves at the beginning of each term to record their progressing skills in both coordination and observation. Do not attempt to make records following every activity!

■ Reflective observations: It is useful to spend regular time reflecting on the progress of a few children (about four children each week). Aim to make some brief comments about each child every half-term.

Informing your planning

Collecting evidence about children's progress is time-consuming but essential. When you are planning, use the information you have collected to help you to decide what learning opportunities you need to provide next for children. For example, a child who has poor pencil or brush control will benefit from more play with dough or construction toys to build the strength of hand muscles.

Example of a recording chart

Name: Henry Wakefield			D.O.B. 26.2.04		Date of entry: 16.4.07	
Term	Personal, Social and Emotional Development	Communication, Language and Literacy	Problem solving, Reasoning and Numeracy	Knowledge and Understanding of the World	Physical Development	Creative Development
ONE	Settles happily when Mum leaves but likes to start his day with familiarity of sand play. 7.5.07 SG	Increasing attention and recall at story times and is happy to join in at circle time. Speaks clearly, and enjoyed making tape recording as a group. 6.6.07 SG	Recognises and names groups of two objects Counts beyond 9. Uses counting in tasks and own play. 18.7.07 LB	Talks about significant own experiences. Asks why and how. Shows keen interest in the computer and a remote control car. 27.6.07 SG	Moves with control and spatial awareness. 28.5.07 SG	Creates 3D models. Enjoyed topic on builders and houses. 18.7.07 LB
TWO						
THREE						

Overview of six-week Plan

Week	Topic Focus	Personal, Social and Emotional Development	Communication, Language and Literacy	Problem Solving, Reasoning and Numeracy	Knowledge and Understanding of the World	Physical Development	Creative Development
1	Exercise and Health	Speaking, sharing ideas, understanding right and wrong	Extending vocabulary, listening to stories and rhymes	Counting, symmetry, comparing and measuring	Investigating, finding out about ICT, recording, talking	Moving with control and coordination, recognising changes in the body	Making and creating, expressing ideas
2	Ball skills	Speaking, listening, working as part of a group, maintaining concentration	Extending vocabulary, writing for different purposes, names and captions	Comparing 3D shapes, estimating, recognising and recreating patterns	Finding out about the environment. Constructing and investigating objects and materials	Using small equipment, moving with confidence	Using their Imagination, exploring papier-mâché and printing
3	Balance and Coordination	Speaking, listening, working with others, being confident to try new activities	Extending vocabulary, attentive listening, listening with enjoyment	Constructing, predicting and reflecting on problems, using positional language	Investigating & exploring ideas, discovering by experience, noticing similarities & differences	Moving in safety, with control and co-ordination, using a range of equipment	Using imagination in music and singing, self-expression through painting
4	Creative Bodies	Awareness of needs of others, considering the impact of their words and actions, concentration	Listening and responding, extending vocabulary	Saying and using numbers, using everyday words to describe position, recognising numbers 1-9	Noticing similarities and differences, observing and investigating, asking questions	Showing an awareness of space, using a range of equipment, moving with confidence & imagination	Responding to what they see and hear, exploring 2 & 3D, using imagination in music and dance
5	Space, Direction and Orientation	Speaking, listening, understanding the need for agreed codes of behaviour	Extending vocabulary, writing for different purposes, interacting with others to negotiate plans	Using mathematical ideas to solve problems, describing positions	Using programmable toys to support their learning, building and constructing	Handling tools with control, using a range of equipment, moving with control and co-ordination	Expressing and communicating ideas, using imagination in art and design, and in music and dance
6	Teamwork and Co-operation	Understanding right and wrong, working as part of a team, forming good relationships	Extending vocabulary, talking to clarify thinking and ideas, attentive listening, responding appropriately	Describing shape and size of solids and flats, comparing quantities, counting reliably to 10	Building and constructing, selecting techniques to assemble and join, finding out about their environment and asking questions	Showing an awareness of space, of themselves and others, using a range of equipment, moving with confidence	Responding to what they see, exploring colour, texture, shape and form in 2 & 3D, using imagination in art and design

Home links

The theme of 'Early Sports Skills' lends itself to links with children's home life and families. Through working together children and adults gain respect for each other and build comfortable and confident relationships.

Establishing partnerships

- Inform parents in advance each week of the next theme to be covered in 'Early Sport Skills'. By understanding the work of the group, parents will be able to enjoy the involvement of contributing ideas, time and resources.
- Position a list of 'resources needed' on the parents' notice board.
- Obtain permission from all parents in advance of any visits. Ensure that all visits are planned thoroughly and risk assessments are carried out.
- Invite parents to the Sports Day event.
- Photocopy the parents' page for each child to take home, and place a copy on the parents' notice board.

Visiting enthusiasts

- Encourage parents to visit the group to demonstrate their sporting skills or to show children their medals, certificates, trophies etc.
- If you have a local and willing sportsperson, ask them to visit and talk about their sport with the children.
- Invite trainers from your local leisure centre to come and demonstrate more unusual sports e.g. Tai Kwondo, Judo, Tai Chi.
- Invite a teacher from your local dance school to come and demonstrate basic dance steps and body movements.

Resource requests

- Ask parents to contribute photographs, pictures and cuttings about sport from magazines and newspapers.
- Ask parents to donate or loan sports equipment, either to use, or for display.
- Set up a collection point for plastic bottles with lids. These can be filled with water or sand and used to depict goal posts, corners of the playing pitch or court.
- Ask for old balls of wool for making pom-poms for your cheerleaders.

Sports Day events

- Enlist the help of a few parents to help with the activities, refreshments and sports events.
- Ask for parents to help put up bunting, arrows and other signage in advance of the Sports Day.

Notes